In memory of my son, Thomas Boyd Abbott, I dedicate this book to:

All the children who shared with me the suffering of physical, mental, sexual and emotional brutality. To those very same boys I met again as an adult, while I served time in Soledad, San Quentin, Folsom and in Oregon state and Washington state penitentiaries.

To the many I have watched slaughtered on those prisons' yards, and to those who went on to kill — three of whom I wrote to often until they were executed by the state that raised them.

To all the incarcerated children, who because of cruel physical beatings, sexual molestations and mental manipulations, become society's outcasts and nonconformists; not because they are bad children but because they have become products of the system.

To the children who are — and will be — growing up as I did, filled with shame and guilt, unable to speak with any member of a society that refuses to lift its head from the sands of ignorance.

To the future victims of these victims.

And to the following men:

George Jackson, shot and killed by guards at San Quentin; Billy Cook, murdered at San Quentin; Gary Gilmore, executed by the state of Utah; Tony Zamore, murdered at San Quentin; Wallace Michael Ford, murdered at Vacaville; Dennis Dimmick, murdered at Vacaville; Jimmy Trembly, murdered at Soledad; Kenny West, shot and killed during a bank robbery; "Joker" Jones, murdered by prison guards at San Quentin; "Wop," murdered by-inmates at San Quentin; Jason, poisoned at Oregon State Penitentiary; and to Charles Manson, a friend whose soul was killed by the system.

— Dwight Edgar Abbott

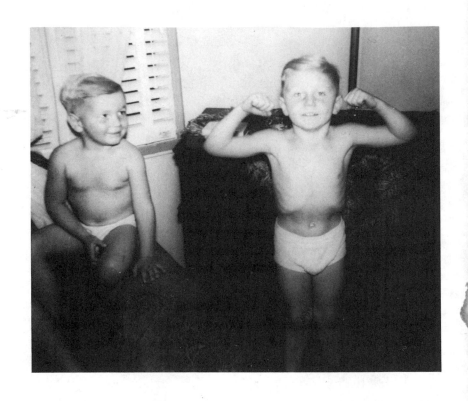

**Danny and Dwight Abbott, 9 years old**

# Introduction

The counselor entered my dorm in juvenile hall late one night. He shook me awake and told me to go into the bathroom. Once there, he told me, "Face the wall." I did as I was told.

The counselor felt for my pajama bottoms and pulled them down. He began to fondle my penis. He turned me around to face him. I watched in horror as he put his mouth on me.

I felt his finger touching my bottom. I cried out in pain as he brutally jammed it inside me. He put his other hand over my mouth to muffle the sound.

This was the beginning of a horrifying experience I've never forgotten. This is the story of a boy, now a man, who was introduced to a world of brutality, rape and perversion at the tender age of 9.

I was sent to Los Angeles County Juvenile Hall after my parents were seriously injured in an automobile accident. I was placed in a dormitory with other young children, ranging in age from 7 to 17. Many of those children were there because of broken families. Others were there because they were criminals.

For a 9-year-old boy who had never been in trouble with the law, juvenile hall quickly became a living nightmare. On the day of my arrival, one of the older black boys beat me severely. A counselor looked on and made no attempt to stop him. That same night, I watched three Mexican boys sexually assault a white boy. The Mexicans were all about 15 years old. The white boy was about 7.

During the four months I was kept at juvenile hall, I experienced my first physical beating, my first sexual molestation, my first placement in solitary confinement, and I watched, for the first time, an act of brutal rape. During this same period, I also committed my first violent act. My victim nearly died.

Now, nearly 50, with most of my 10-year sentence for assault behind me, I write my story with the hope that young people in trouble — or headed that way — might be saved from what awaits them behind the locked doors of America's juvenile halls and reform schools.

At this moment, a young boy or girl is being physically, sexually, mentally, and emotionally mistreated within the walls of America's juvenile penal system. This abuse comes not only from the children's peers but from the people whom society has entrusted with the children's welfare. These assaults will brutally scar the tender and impressionable innocents.

These children will eventually respond to their pain by stealing, raping and murdering.

When I reached the legally determined age of responsibility, I had become a predator, having learned how not to become a victim. Incarcerated children are constantly told what to do and when to do it — when to eat, when to sleep, when to talk, when to use the bathroom, when to sit, when to stand. Consequently, I never learned how to make a decision in a healthy manner common to children raised in a family environment. After my first incarceration, at Los Angeles County Juvenile Hall, by the time Dad left the hospital and had me released, I was no longer the child he and my mother had raised.

I now understand, that because of my feelings of guilt and rage, I lied to my parents and the many shrinks who tried to analyze me. I tried to confuse those who tried to help me. My shame has been bottled up inside me for my entire life, and only now am I willing to share it with anyone.

If I can help one troubled child, or can awaken one adult to the reality of what really occurs behind those walls, then perhaps, the years of my life behind bars will have not been entirely wasted.

Dwight Edgar Abbott
California State Prison, Folsom
December 1990

# ONE

As childhoods go, mine was not remarkable or unusual until I reached 9 years of age. I was born in Alhambra, California, on Oct. 4, 1942. At that time, my home was in El Monte, on Durfee Road. Few people called me Dwight. They knew me as Sonny, as friends and family do today.

It is difficult for me to remember what my life was like before the age of 9. But I do recall that when I was 5, my brother Danny and I were playing outside, near the house. Our parents were gone, and Roberta — my mother's sister — was drunk as usual. Roberta made it a point to never pay attention to what we did.

There was an old washing machine in back of the house. It had an electrically operated clothes wringer attached to it. I filled the machine's tub with water and, as I sat inside it, soaked my pants and stuffed them through the wringer.

I was having a great time, until somehow I caught my finger in the clothing. My hand and arm followed the pants through the wringer. It broke my arm and several fingers.

The woman next door heard me screaming. She rescued me by reversing the wringer. Mom and Dad returned home and rushed me to the hospital.

I remember crying until the doctor put me to sleep. When I woke and saw a big cast covering my arm and hand, I started to cry all over again.

There were five kids in the family. Mother had had David, Reid and Carolyn from a previous marriage. My parents married in 1941, and I was born a year later. Danny arrived 14 months after me.

As I said, Roberta was my mother's sister. She took care of the kids and the house most of the time. My parents were busy with their metal-finishing business. Roberta was busy being an alcoholic.

Dad was a compulsive gambler, yet he always provided well for the family. He worked hard; we had all we needed, and then some. Once their business became successful, Mom and Dad began taking trips to Las Vegas almost every weekend. They left all us kids in Roberta's care.

Whenever they were gone, Roberta would really hit the booze. We ran around hungry and dirty, most often uncared for. Our food — whatever we could open — we ate cold. Roberta's importance now is due to the fact that her care — or lack of it — was what eventually caused me to be confined to Los Angeles County Juvenile Hall.

My parents' business grew and grew, and soon they built another shop, on Merced Avenue in El Monte. At that time, they were also preparing to move the family to Covina, where Dad was having a new home built. It was located in an orange grove. It even had a swimming pool.

The entire family began going to Las Vegas together, spending weekends on Lake Mead while Dad gambled. I was never unhappy during this period. In fact, I was spoiled. It seemed I was Dad's favorite. Danny was Mom's favorite.

Dad enjoyed fishing, and his brother owned a boat dock and a cafe on the Colorado River, at Willow Beach, on the Arizona side of Boulder Dam. I loved to fish there, too, but there was another reason why I looked forward to going there each weekend. I had made friends with one of the many wild burros at the beach.

The burro was as wild as the rest, but somehow he had acquired one heck of a taste for beer. He had come up to me one day while I sat on the dock, drinking a soda. I held the bottle out to the burro. He sniffed it then tossed his head back in disdain.

He continued standing there, staring at me, so I reached inside the cooler and pulled out a bottle of beer. I opened it and held it up to the burro's mouth. The burro sniffed the bottle, then licked it. I tipped the bottle, and the burro sucked it dry.

It was not long before I had given him every beer in the cooler. He was one drunk burro. Watching him stagger away was the funniest thing I had ever seen.

The burro and I did this each time I went to Willow Beach, for at least a year. One time the burro didn't show, and I never saw him again.

I did well in school. I made good grades and had many friends. I joined in with all the school activities. Most of my friends were boys because at that age, most of us just stood around sneering at the girls. I had no idea how girls felt about me.

Shortly after my 9th birthday, my secure, happy and comfortable world fell apart.

My parents had taken another trip to Las Vegas with some family friends. Again, they left us all with Roberta. As usual, she was drunk.

It was early in the evening, as I recall, and we were all sitting on the living room floor, eating cereal from the box. We ate it dry, since the milk in the icebox had turned sour. Roberta was passed out on the sofa, where she spent most of her time.

There was a knock at the front door. Reid opened it. There was the woman from next door, standing with her husband. Reid invited them in.

The man said, "We need to speak with Roberta."

We pointed to the couch, and they tried to wake her. That proved impossible. The man became angry and shouted at her, then he rolled her onto the floor. Roberta kept snoring.

The woman was upset, too. She had been crying since they entered the house. The man stood over us, looking down, then took us to their house. We left Roberta where she was, on the floor.

Danny and I had not had a bath in two days. The woman gave us one, then dressed us in the clean clothes we had carried with us from our house. She fed us a hot meal. The woman was very kind.

After we ate, we sat in front of the television. Then, there was a knock at the door. The man opened it, and I saw two police officers standing on the porch. They spoke quietly with the man. I could not hear what they were saying.

The woman walked to the television and turned it off. She

looked at us and said, "The nice police officers want to speak with you."

During the many years since that night, I have had contact with hundreds of cops. That night was the only time I ever saw one with tears in his eyes. The cop had a difficult time saying what he needed to tell us, but as we stood there on the porch, we learned Mom and Dad had been seriously injured in an auto accident, near Pasadena.

Being so young, the seriousness of the police officer's words did not immediately affect me. The severity of the situation took hold once we arrived at the hospital. At first, the hospital workers told us we could not see our parents. But when we all began to cry, we were allowed into the room.

"Your parents are asleep," one nurse said. "They won't be awake for awhile."

When I saw my parents, each bandaged from head to foot with thick white gauze, I suddenly realized they had been hurt badly. At that point in my life, death had not yet become a part of my experience, though I heard that a grandfather of mine put a gun to his head.

We spent the night at the neighbor's house, and in the morning some people came to the house. They said they were going to take us away because Roberta was unable to care for us.

Danny did not go to Los Angeles County Juvenile Hall, as I did, in what was to be a temporary stay. To this day, I do not know where they took Carolyn, Reid and David.

# TWO

Los Angeles County Juvenile Hall terrified me. From the outside, I saw nothing but a tremendous wall. Stepping out of the car, I looked up at that wall. One of the social workers, a tall, thickly built man, led me to a large metal door. I heard the lock click from the inside. It opened slowly, and the man nudged me through that doorway and into a small, white-tiled room.

I can only dimly remember how I was processed into the hall and the dormitory. I know I was fingerprinted, and a man took my picture. I was also given a set of county-issued clothing before being led to the dorm.

A counselor walked with me across a narrow yard to a large building. The lock clicked open from the inside of that door, too. I stepped through the doorway. The noise was deafening.

There was a fight going on just a few feet from where the counselor and I stood. He completely ignored it. Kids were yelling, running all over the place.

Two rows of beds flanked my right side, with about 20 beds in each row. To my left was an office from which another counselor was just leaving. Across from the counselor's office was another door. I learned later that it led to the shower area.

The counselor who had walked me to the dorm took me by the arm and scooted me to his office. In a firm voice, he told me about the rules, all of which were being violated when we entered the dorm. There was to be no loud noise, no smoking and no fighting, he said.

We left his office and walked to the bed he had assigned to me. "Make it up before you do anything else," he said. A moment later, I made my first mistake. I took the blankets and sheets the counselor had given me and laid them on the bed next to mine. A black boy, twice my size and several years older, picked up the bedding and threw it on the floor.

"Watch where you put that, boy," he said. I looked at him but said nothing. I'd never seen a black person before. He scared me to death.

Seeing the other boys watching, he shoved me and asked, "What do you think you're doing?"

I was about to tell him when he took a step forward and hit me square on the mouth.

He'd knocked me to the floor and, along with the pain, I laid there, a very frightened and confused little boy. The black boy began kicking me, and I did my best to cover my head. This went on for what seemed like minutes before a counselor pulled him away from me.

I stood and, crying, saw the other kids watching me. My nose was swollen and bleeding.

"You'll be all right," the counselor said. "You better learn not to mess with anyone. Stop being such a baby."

I was completely confused. I'd never been hit before in my life, much less with a closed fist. I couldn't stop crying, so the counselor slapped me so hard that I rolled over my bed and onto the cold floor.

"You better fight next time," he said. "I'm not here to babysit you."

That evening, as I learned was done every night after returning from supper, everyone undressed and stood in front of their bed, a towel wrapped around themselves, until it was their turn to shower. Five kids showered at a time, while a counselor sat at one the tables near us, making sure no one spoke.

He should have been more concerned with what was going on in the shower room.

When it was my turn, I walked into the shower room and saw a couple of older kids holding a young white boy, about my age. He was bent over in front of a black kid, who had his penis inside the little boy's bottom. A Mexican kid held his hand over the boy's mouth, but I could still hear him crying. The bigger kids were about 15 years old. Each time the young boy struggled, one of them hit him on the back of his head.

At my age, it was difficult, if not impossible, to understand what was happening. I thought the boy was being punished for something he had done. I knew nothing about sex, of any sort.

I showered quickly, saying nothing to them. Even at that age, I knew instinctively it was best to keep to myself. I had already been beaten badly that day. I had no desire to make anyone mad at me again.

When the entire dorm had showered, the counselors allowed us to sit at tables and talk, or we could lay on our beds until the lights-out call. I stayed close to my bed. Another fight broke out between two of the older children. The counselor let it continue for some time before he broke it up.

When the lights went out, I laid on my bed and cried into my pillow until I fell asleep. I never needed Mom and Dad as badly as I did that night. More than anything, I wanted to go home.

The next day was the same as the first. The noise and fighting were continuous. The older, stronger kids raped the younger ones, who were unable to defend against the attacks.

I cannot honestly say that all the counselors allowed the fights, nor can I say for sure how many knew of the rapes and allowed them to occur. I do know that two counselors not only allowed those things to happen but also encouraged them. Their names were Mr. Alexander, a black man, and Mr. Beeman, a white.

Mr. Alexander would arrange bare-fisted fights, giving cigarettes to the winner. I also watched him observe, from beginning to end, black kids raping white ones.

On my third night at juvenile hall, I was sleeping soundly when Mr. Beeman shook me awake.

He whispered, "I want to talk to you in the bathroom." I had already learned I'd better do what a counselor told me or risk getting punched. I got out of bed and walked to the bathroom. I hoped Mr. Beeman had good news to tell me about my parents. Since my arrival, no one had mentioned them.

I walked into the bathroom. Mr. Beeman closed the door behind us. He took my arm and walked me to the far end of the room. He pushed me face-first against the wall and pulled my underwear down.

"Step out of them," he said.

He played with my penis until it became erect. Then he placed his mouth on it and copulated me for a short time, as I watched in fear and confusion. I felt his finger touching my bottom. I cried out in pain as he jammed his finger inside me, and he put his other hand over my mouth and muffled the sound.

I had no idea why he was doing that. I had done nothing wrong. I was very frightened, but I stopped crying so he wouldn't hit me.

"Lay down on the floor," he said.

I laid on my stomach. With his fingers, he rubbed something cold and wet on my rectum. Again, Mr. Beeman put his finger inside me. I tried to get away from him, and he slapped me.

"Don't move," he said.

I looked over my shoulder and saw he had his pants opened. He was rubbing his penis with something from a small can. I started crying, and he reached down and clamped his hand over my mouth so hard that my lips began to bleed. I couldn't breathe and began to panic. I cannot describe the pain of this man ramming his penis inside me, and I seem to be feeling it all over again now as I write this. Never before had I experienced such pain, not even when my arm went through that washing-machine wringer.

Mr. Beeman made strange moaning sounds, then pulled himself out of me and stood. He yanked me up toward him, keeping his hand over my mouth until I stopped crying.

"Put it on," he said, handing me my underwear.

He wiped himself off with a towel then took me to his office. He sat on the edge of his desk and, pointing his finger at me, whispered, "If you ever say anything to anyone about what just happened, I'll make sure you never go home. Now get to bed."

I believed every word he told me, and it has taken nearly forty years now to mention what occurred that night. I walked out of the office, went to my bed and cried myself to sleep.

In the morning, I awoke and walked to the bathroom. Two kids there began snickering and pointed to my bottom. I reached behind me and felt dampness on my underwear. In a toilet stall, I pulled my underwear down and saw a large spot of blood. When I returned to my bed, I pulled another set of shorts from the small dresser and put them on. I was afraid someone would find out what happened. Then I would not go home.

That night, I was in the shower when the black kid who'd beaten me up walked over. Two Mexican boys were with him. They began hitting me, and I began to cry, loudly. I knew the counselor in the dorm area heard me, but he did not come to see what the problem was.

The black kid was grabbing me, trying to hold me still. I felt one of the Mexicans feeling my bottom. Somehow, I broke loose from the black kid's grasp. I ran out of the shower room.

I returned to my bed and was sitting there, catching my breath, when the black kid walked up to me.

"I'm gonna get some of that," he said, pointing to my bottom. "Better not say nothin', boy."

He walked away. I laid down on my bed and thought, "Daddy, what's happening to me?"

Sometime the next week, the counselors took us all out to a field across the compound for recreation. The counselors chose which kids would be on the teams, and a softball game began.

My team was in the field first. We made three easy outs then walked to the backstop fence for our turns to hit. When it was my turn, I swung a thick, wooden bat a few times to loosen my arms then stepped to the plate. I looked behind me and saw that the black kid who'd beaten me was playing catcher.

For the moment, I wasn't concerned with him. I felt he wouldn't bother me while the counselors were there. I was wrong. As the black kid crouched near the ground, he looked at me with a grin on his face.

The pitcher tossed the first ball. I set myself to swing and felt a hard pinch on my bottom. I ignored it.

As I waited for the second pitch, he did it again. I turned to look at the boy. He winked. I looked back to the pitcher, and I felt the black kid pinch me again.

A sudden rage fell over me, and I turned and brought the bat down onto the top of his head. I put all my strength into that swing. I pounded him several times more, but I remember most that first strike. I can still feel the warm blood that spurted from his head onto my bare chest and arms.

When one of the counselors tried to stop me, I hit him too. Another counselor grabbed me from behind and pinned my arms. Mr. Alexander yanked the bat from my hands, and I looked down at the black kid. I felt a little sorry for him. I learned later he nearly died.

The counselors took me to solitary confinement, where I soon thought I'd go crazy. Maybe I did, in a way. Solitary confinement consisted of a semi-soundproof cell with a bed, sink and toilet. There was a small, metal flap in the solid steel door that could be opened only from the outside. Counselors used it to look into the cell. Guards used it for feeding.

Twice daily that great event would occur. Breakfast was always a bowl of oatmeal, two pieces of cold toast and a cup of warm milk. Late at night, I received beans, two pieces of stale bread and an apple or orange. The meals were served 17 hours apart.

I had no idea how many other kids were in solitary confinement, but we were all awakened at 5:30 a.m. and served breakfast shortly after. A half hour later, a man came through and picked up the bowls. Each boy then was taken individually from his cell and given a shower, alone.

After returning from my shower, I would find that my mattress and blanket had been removed, placed on the floor outside my cell. It would be returned to me at 10 p.m.

I was not allowed any reading material, and the only clothing I wore were jockey shorts and socks. I saw a person only when I was fed, showered and counted. During that time, they refused to speak with me. At no time did I see or hear anyone else inside the solitary unit.

I stayed there for three months. Then, one day, a guard opened the door of the cell and threw me my clothes. His voice was the first I had heard in all that time.

"Your father's here to take you home," he said.

I stood still, frightened. I was unwilling, and unable, to leave the cell where I had sat for 90 days, staring at the walls, seeing no one, convinced that Mom and Dad had forgotten about me, no longer wanting me. I thought if they had wanted me, I would have gone home long before. I thought the counselor was trying to trick me.

He walked into my cell, helped me put my clothes on and led me from the building. I stepped out into the bright sunlight and had to shield my eyes from the sun while we walked to the waiting room. As I breathed the fresh air, I realized I had never before felt so suddenly alive.

Some things about my early life I have forgotten, but I have not forgotten that afternoon; the brightness of the sun, the freshness of the air. The memory remains with me as if it was yesterday. We walked into the waiting room, and I saw Dad. I stood looking at him. I watched a puzzled expression come over his face. Years later, I recalled that look when Dad told me that his eyes told him I was his son, but that mine had told him that his son was no longer there. My father died feeling that had he not dismissed that strange sensation he experienced then, his son's life would have turned out differently.

Dad was quite correct in believing that he was no longer looking at the well-behaved, polite, loving son he had raised. What he saw was a walking time bomb, ready to explode. It took the County of Los Angeles about four months to construct me, behind the walls surrounding that munitions-manufacturing plant they call juvenile hall.

From the first day I returned home until the day they died, my parents suffered from my actions. Unconsciously, I sought revenge. People I had not yet met were going to suffer, too, at my hands.

# THREE

At last, the five of us kids were back home. Mom was still in the hospital, though. Her injuries had been more serious than Dad's. The day I returned from juvenile hall, Dad took me to see her.

In the hospital room, seeing her laying there with her legs in traction, I saw and felt the pain she had endured, not only from the accident itself but from the many operations afterward. When we walked into the room, she was smiling, and I was happy to learn she would be okay again soon.

The accident had occurred when a doctor, who was driving drunk, crossed the yellow dividing line and smashed head-on into Dad's car. The doctor died instantly; my father died slowly. I learned shortly after his death that the accident had permanently damaged his heart, causing his early death.

My dad drove me to a junkyard and showed me the remains of our car. I later reflected on how anyone survived at all. The engine had been pushed into the front seat, crushing my parents' legs and chests. Their two friends had been asleep in the back seat and had walked away with few injuries.

Throughout my life, I have thought it strange that none of my brothers or sister discussed the accident or, perhaps more importantly, what each of us had experienced while our parents were in the hospital.

At the time, being 9 years old, I felt as if no one cared where I had been or what I had experienced. I was upset with my family for not caring. I had become so emotionally disturbed as a direct result of my experience at juvenile hall that, without realizing it, I blamed my entire family for my pain and anguish.

I was having a difficult time making friends with the other kids. I rebelled against Dad, disobeying him. I was determined to not do what I was asked, or ordered, to do. No one truly understood the root cause of my behavior. Dad called it a "phase" and attributed it to rebelling against authority.

The actual truth had become well hidden under layers of anger, guilt and resentment. I had become so afraid and spiteful of authority figures while at juvenile hall that it had carried over to everyone at home. There was no way Dad could understand that I was acting out a serious emotional problem, rather than simply going through a stage of life. His punishments served only to feed my emotional distress.

My brother Danny and I had always been very close. We had always shared our things and had spent much time together. But our relationship came to an abrupt end soon after I returned home.

I no longer wanted him or anyone else near me. I began to wander off by myself. Rather than play near the house in the afternoons, as I had done before, I would stay at school as long as I could, sitting by myself on the grass at the playground. Rarely did I play with my school buddies. That always seemed to end in a fight, especially when I felt I was being roughed up by a bigger kid.

My grades fell from B's and C's to D's and F's. I skipped classes. And when I did go, I refused to do what the teacher asked. If a teacher asked why I wasn't paying attention, I wouldn't respond. I'd sit there at my little desk and stare out the window or look at the floor. Again and again, school administrators punished me for being a brat and, when I got home, my parents punished me again, since the teacher would call and describe what had happened.

The more I was punished, the more I hid within myself. I refused to allow anyone, or anything, ever make me feel pain again. And all during this time, I felt great pain inside.

One day, close to my 11th birthday, all my feelings that I thought I had controlled came to the surface. For the first time, Dad saw the anger inside me.

An older and bigger boy at school had decided to pick on me. I was still small in size and appeared a good target for bullies. I was walking home from school when this bully approached me and began shoving me around. He took my spelling book, tore it in half then shoved me to the ground.

I got up and ran from him. By the time I got home, I was crying. Dad was there on the porch. He yelled to the bully, telling him to leave me alone. I ran inside the house and went straight to my room. I stayed there until Dad talked me into eating dinner.

The next morning, I went to the garage and found a piece of wood, a 2-by-4 that was about 3 feet long. I took the board outside and leaned it against a bush in front of our house.

I stood there, waiting for the bully. Eventually he appeared, and as soon as he saw me, he shouted, "Momma's boy" and a few other things I did not care for. I kept quiet and stood still. He approached me and gave me a shove. I backed up a step, reached for the board and, with two hands, began hitting him with it.

He cried and yelled, and the louder he yelled, the harder I hit him. People across the street were watching us. A man ran over and took the board away from me. Then I saw the kid's father running for me, and I ran into my house. No one inside knew what had happened as I hid in my bedroom.

A few moments passed before I heard a banging at the front door, and then a muffled conversation. Someone said the word "police." My dad walked into my room and found me hiding under my bed.

"Go to the living room," he said. I walked in and saw two cops standing near the front door.

"What happened?" one asked.

"I'm tired of that bully picking on me," I said. "If it ever happens again, I'll kill him."

Dad confirmed the story, telling the police he had to yell at the kid the day before. Dad agreed to pay the boy's medical bills, and the matter was forgotten.

At least it seemed to me everyone else had forgotten it. I was not punished, although I waited several days for a spanking.

I began to steal not long after that incident.

At a pet shop down the street, there was a puppy I had fallen in love with. I did not have the $5 needed to buy her. In those days, that was an incredible amount of money for a child to have.

I hadn't planned to steal. It just happened without me giving any thought to it. I walked to a nearby house and knocked on the front door. When no one answered, I went around back and found the door opened. I entered the house and found a large jar in a closet. It was filled with silver dollars. I took five of them and left.

I went to the pet shop, bought the dog, and named her Ginger. When I got home, I told Dad I had found her wandering around. He called the newspaper and placed an advertisement for the "lost" dog. I knew no one would claim her.

A few days later, much to my surprise, a man and woman came to our house. They looked at Ginger and told Dad she was indeed the dog they had lost.

I knew they were lying, obviously, but I was unable to tell Dad. I had to let the man and woman take Ginger, but I mentally marked one more notch against authority figures.

Dad bought me another puppy. She looked just like Ginger, and I named her that, too. She and I romped and played together for many hours, but I lost her too when she was run over and killed while I was away, having another go at juvenile hall.

# FOUR

I had just turned 12 when my rebellion returned me to Los Angeles County Juvenile Hall.

Three years had passed since my first stay there. So much of what I had become as a result had gone from bad to worse. I had constant problems with the police. For a while, Mom and Dad had been able to solve my problems and keep me at home. The stupid things I was doing were not the acts of a boy gone bad. They were, as I see now, pleas for help. But my distrust had convinced me not to reach out to others.

I wanted so much to be the little man of the house. I wanted my parents to be proud of me. Yet I knew they would be ashamed of me if I told them my experiences at the hall.

My stepbrother David did not help matters, either. His actions intensified my already serious problems. Even at home I was confronted with a situation I found very similar to that of the hall.

One day, in the orange grove behind the house, David tried to molest me. When I didn't participate in his plan, he fell into a rage and began beating me. From that day on, David hit me just for the hell of it. Sometimes he would slap me and other times he would beat me with his closed fists. I never told anyone about the attacks, but one day I reached my limit. I walked into Dad's bedroom and loaded his shotgun. I was going to kill my stepbrother. Fortunately, he had left the house. I put the shotgun back in Dad's closet.

When David returned, he approached me in the backyard and slapped me for no reason. I warned him that I'd tell Dad if he ever did it again. That caused him to get angrier, and he beat me badly. When I got myself away from him, I ran into the house and locked myself in my bedroom. I cried for hours, then decided to run away.

I stepped into the hall, and heard David taking a shower. I left the house and jumped into David's car, a stick shift. Because he always left his keys in the ignition, I was able to start the engine and pull away from the house. I did not yet know how to drive, other than how to go forward in first gear.

I drove the car for about 30 miles before the engine overheated and blew up. I continued my journey on foot.

Across the road, I saw two unoccupied houses. I broke into both. I found two pistols in the second house and took them with me. I continued down the road and walked a very long time. I was hungry and tired, but knew I could not go home. David would kill me.

The next thing I did was very stupid. I walked into a police station, resolved to tell them of all the crimes I had committed. I wanted them to protect me from my stepbrother.

I walked up to the desk sergeant. "Can I help you?" he asked. I reached under my shirt and pulled out one of the pistols I had stolen, intending to give it to him.

A cop across the room shouted, "Look out! He's got a gun!"

Another yelled, "My God! He's just a kid!"

Three cops grabbed me and threw me to the floor, breaking my arm in the process. They grabbed the guns and immediately drove me to a hospital, where my arm was set and cast. Later that night, an officer took me to Juvenile Hall. They processed me through to the same dorm I was in during my first stay.

Though I was scared, I was determined this time not to do anything I didn't want to.

That first night, an older kid beat me up, just to let me know he was in charge. After the others went to sleep, I got out of bed, walked to a card table and picked up a folding metal chair.

I saw a counselor watching me from his office window, but by the time he realized what I was going to do, it was too late.

"Put that chair down!" he shouted, running out of the office.

I had already reached the bully's bed. I brought the chair down with all my strength, hitting him square on the face. Later,

I learned I had broken his cheek bone and several ribs. The counselor wrestled the chair from my grasp.

My greatest satisfaction, besides watching the bully lay under his bed, was that he began to cry, loudly. Everyone heard him.

The counselor took me straight to solitary confinement. That did not bother me. Nothing did anymore.

Two days later, I appeared before the court. I saw Mom and Dad sitting together on a bench across the room. The judge told me I was allowed to sit with them, and I did.

For a moment, it seemed the judge was going to release me to their custody. Mom was crying, pleading with the judge to give me another chance. A counselor stood and described to the court what I had done to the bully. He forgot to mention that the kid was five years older than me, twice my size, and that he had beat me up for no better reason than to prove he was the dorm leader.

Nothing was said in my defense, though my attitude did not help matters. When the judge asked me about the fight, I didn't answer him. This 12-year-old boy had given up hope.

The court ruled to keep me in the care of Juvenile Hall until my "best interest" was decided. Sending me home was certainly not the ideal answer, but what was? Sending me back to Juvenile Hall would only make matters worse.

When a counselor led me from the courtroom, I was too afraid to show my pain. I did not look back at my parents. I had already learned that showing emotions was a sign of weakness. Weakness invited abuse from everyone.

Walking back across the yard toward solitary confinement with two counselors holding my arms, I saw for what seemed the first time the trees, bushes, grass and flowers that surrounded the compound. An intense feeling within me surfaced. Suddenly, I wanted to run across the grass, smell the flowers and climb the trees. I just wanted to be the kid I was and the kid I used to be, smiling, laughing, playing.

Little did I know that my chance for anything resembling a normal life had already been lost. I would never be a kid again.

Alone in my cell late that night, I felt safe, knowing that I could cry and go unheard. But I was wrong.

After an hour or so, a counselor opened my cell door. He asked, "Can I help you?"

That was the first time anyone there had spoken kindly to me, but I didn't answer him. The counselor walked to my bed. He sat down and put his arm around me. I flinched, but he held me tighter.

"It's okay to cry," he said. "I understand."

He left without saying another word. The next night, he came to my cell again. He gave me a doughnut, saying, "If you need someone to talk to, I'll be glad to listen and help."

The counselor came to my cell several nights in a row. During the day, I was alone, with nothing to do but sit and stare at a wall or walk back and forth on the cold floor. At night, the counselor would bring me a kind word and something to eat. I began to anticipate the nights, so he would come and make me feel like someone cared.

At one point, he didn't come by for two days. That made me cry. I figured he had given up on me too. I didn't know he'd taken two days off work until he returned and entered my cell.

"What do you want the most?" he asked.

I looked at him and said, "I want to go home."

Then, like a broken dam, I burst into tears. He sat beside me and held me, like Mom used to do. Then I felt his hand in a place Mom wouldn't have put hers. He pulled my underwear down, and as I tried to pull myself away from him, he held me tighter.

"I can arrange for you to go home," he said.

I had no doubt he could let me out of solitary and get me home. After all, he had the keys. Yet, even believing that, I continued to struggle. I wanted him to stop touching me.

"If you sit still and be good, I'll take you home when I go to my house," he said. "I've already called your parents and told them I'd do it. They said they won't sleep until you arrive."

I sat still.

"Everything's going to be fine," he said, smiling. He continued to fondle me, one hand on my penis, the other on my bottom.

"Stand up," he said. I did as I was told. He turned me so my back was toward him. He was still sitting on my bed. I felt him trying to put his finger in my behind.

"It hurts," I said.

"I'll be right back."

He stood then walked out of the cell, leaving the cell door open. I looked out and, for some reason, felt assured he was really going to take me home. I was frightened, because I knew he was going to do something to me. But he had promised he wouldn't hurt me, and I believed him. What he had already done was something I didn't like, but as long as he didn't hurt me, and took me home, I was willing to let him do whatever he wanted.

He returned, holding something in his hand. I didn't know what it was, but I figured it was similar to what the other counselor had used on me.

"Stand there, and face the wall," he said. Again, I did as I was told. He wiped some of the cream on my behind, and I felt his finger go inside me. It hurt a little bit. I tried to step away from him, and he grabbed my shoulder. "If you want to go home, you better stand still."

I did as I was told. Then, I felt something much larger than his finger touch my butt. I reached behind me to push it away, but he reached around me and pinned my arms to my side. He pushed me hard against the cell wall hard enough to split my lip open. He forced his penis into me.

"It hurts!" I yelled.

All I heard were the strange noises the counselor made. When he pulled out of me, I started to cry. I touched my bottom and saw blood on my hand.

I quit crying then asked, "Can I go home now?"

"Lay down on the mattress. I want to talk to you."

I pulled on my underwear and laid on the mattress, like he told me to do. He pulled my underwear down and touched my penis.

"I won't let you put that in me again," I said.

"I won't," he said. Instead, he orally copulated me, for a long time. He said, "As soon as you do to me what I just did to you, you'll go home." I told him there was no way I was going to put my mouth on him. He tried to force my head down to his lap.

"I'll bite you," I said. He let go of my head. He stood, pulled on his pants and walked out of the cell. All that night, I waited for him to come and get me, to take me home. I never saw him again.

Another counselor came to my cell in the morning to take out my mattress. I knew by then that I had made a tremendous mistake. I convinced myself it was my fault the counselor hadn't taken me home. After all, he said he'd take me home if I did to him what he had done to me.

A few weeks later, another counselor escorted me to his office. He introduced me to a man named Mr. Burger. Mr. Burger said he'd heard about me from the juvenile court.

"I want to talk to you," he said. I sat on a chair opposite from him. "Would you like to go live at the Optimist Home for Boys?"

"Where's that?"

"It's in Highland Park," he said. "You won't be locked up there, like you are here. If you agree to go, you'll come with me today."

It sounded much better than where I had been, but before I agreed, I asked, "What do you want me to do for you?"

Mr. Burger gave me a puzzled look. After a moment, he said, "All I want is for you to be a good boy and not cause any trouble."

I agreed to go, and he took me to the home that afternoon, just as he had promised. And I didn't have to let him do anything to me, either.

# FIVE

As we rode in the car up the driveway leading to the boys' home, I saw a three-story house at the bottom of a small hill.

"The boys who are 14 to 17 live there for now," Mr. Burger said. "The younger boys live farther up the hill, in a brand new building. All the boys eat here at the house. The new dining room is still being built."

He pointed to another building still under construction. "That's a new dorm for the older kids. That one next to it is the dining hall. When this is all completed, the whole hill will be covered with one, single-story building." Behind it, he said, on an even higher hill, was yet more construction — two apartment units.

Mr. Burger said one of the units was for himself and one was for a woman I later called Sewing Lady. I can't recall her name, but she spent every daylight hour in her sewing room, repairing the children's clothes. She was a very old woman, and she had a lot of love in her heart for all the kids.

To the right of the three-story house was a large, barn-like structure. Mr. Burger said it was the gymnasium. Above that was the workshop.

Mr. Burger introduced me to the superintendent, Mr. Brawley. I thought he seemed a kindly old man, who anyone might want for a father or grandfather. I later learned how deceiving first impressions can be.

I cannot recall the houseparents' names. They were a married couple who cared for us like we were their own children. I have fond memories of them both. They were always there when we needed them.

The junior dorm housed 40 kids; senior dorm had 30. I enjoyed my life there, for a while. I attended school, right across the street from the home. I met my first girlfriend there. Her par-

ents allowed her to visit me at the home on weekends. And my
parents visited me every week. But I could still not talk to them
about all the feelings that needed to be shared. I was too
ashamed, and they had no idea how to get me to communicate.

When they visited, the three of us would walk the grounds.
Mom and Dad did all the talking. I remained quiet, withdrawn. I
would only answer their more casual questions. I could not talk
about myself. When "I" was brought into the conversation, I
quickly changed the subject.

At the boys' home, it was soon apparent I was quite the loner.
That seemed to offend some people, but it made others curious
enough to try to get inside my head.

The gymnasium became my second home. After I finished
my chores, I was there. There was a drive within me that made
me try to become bigger and in better shape than the others.

Over the weeks, I saw changes in my physique, and began to
feel better about myself. Once skinny and weak, I became firm
and solid, with strong muscles. Puberty arrived, which confused
me even more. No one, not even my father, had ever clued me in
about sex, or what was happening to me. Working out took my
mind off other problems.

One of the home's counselors often coached us. We called
him Jungle Jim. He was a decent sort, although he had a very bad
temper. It showed itself when he felt he had been crossed. Jim
was often too harsh with discipline, especially when he caught a
boy breaking the rules of the home.

One day, instead of raking the yard, I was working out on the
trampoline. Jungle Jim found me in the gym and started yelling at
me. When I jumped down to the floor, he slapped me hard, and
sent me reeling backward. As quickly as he lost control, he
regained it.

"Sorry, Sonny," he said.

I stared at him and remained silent. I was determined not to
cry. After this incident Jim befriended me. At first, I thought he
was another guy who wanted to take me to the bathroom. He
was always trying to put his arm on my shoulder. And I would

always pull away. I finally told him I didn't appreciate him touching me. He never did it again.

I began working out on the speed bag but was having trouble with my coordination. Jim saw me struggle, and began to give me boxing lessons. He was a good instructor, and I was grimly determined to defend myself. The bigger kids were already harassing me. It was a matter of time before things really went down. But I was a fast learner, the best student Jungle Jim ever had.

After a few months of training with Jim, my movements became quick. I learned how to put my weight behind a punch. Jim and I sparred almost every day, sneaking in time when no one was around. It was against the rules for an employee to strike any of the kids, even in the boxing ring.

Jim taught me how to take punches when I was not fast enough to avoid them, punches that a few months before would have knocked me on my butt. Day by day, my confidence grew. I began to feel better about myself. I walked around with less fear than I ever had before.

And I knew that soon I would put an end to the "accidental" bumps I received, walking to and from the chow hall.

Jungle Jim, somehow, had known what I needed, and he gave it to me. I have no doubt he understood my problem, the shell I created because of fearing others. To this day, I appreciate that man's help, and the confidence he instilled in me. I regret lettting him down, abusing what he had taught me.

Once, I was punching the speed bag when I was set upon from behind by a bully who lived in the junior dorm with me. His creeping up on me proved what I had suspected, that my dedication to improving my body and learning how to fight was threatening to the kids who thought they were Top Dog.

I sensed the bully creeping up on me, but thought he was Jungle Jim, and so continued with the bag. The bully's blow to the back of my head was so unexpected that it slammed me against the bag before I fell to the floor. I was kicked in the face before I could regain my footing. My first instinct was to run, and that is what I did, to the equipment room, where I intended to grab a baseball bat. Halfway there I realized that I no longer needed a bat, and returned to face the bully.

I found him back at the gym, and he kicked out toward me. I blocked his foot with my arm, then hit him hard enough to lift his feet off the ground, knocking him to the floor.

My hand stung badly. I saw one of his teeth stuck in my knuckle.

The bully was down, and I should have walked away. The fight was over. Instead, I lost control. Suddenly, I felt everything — the times I'd been beaten, shoved, raped, abused — and these feelings boiled over. I picked the tooth from my knuckle and then beat that bully to a bloody mess.

By the time I came back to reality, Jungle Jim was screaming into my ear, telling me to get myself together. I looked down at the other boy, feeling nothing; neither satisfaction or regret.

That day, at that hour, I became the predator rather than the prey.

Jungle Jim walked me back to the junior dorm and told me to sit in the dayroom area. I waited 20 minutes for the superintendent. When Mr. Brawley finally appeared, I quickly learned he was not the kind, grandfatherly type he appeared to be when we first met. He told me to stay where I was sitting, and dismissed the other kids to their beds.

Without a word of warning, he hit me with his closed fist, right on my mouth. The impact sent me and the chair backwards, to the floor. The punch broke one of my front teeth in half.

He grabbed my shirt and pulled me from the floor. He slapped me several times then hit me again with a closed fist. Again I fell.

"How do you like getting beat up, boy?" he yelled, pulling my hair. "Not quite as fun as beating up others, is it?"

I swallowed the intense pain and refused to cry. That angered him. He slapped me again, shouting, "Cry, you little bastard!"

I wouldn't. I had cried myself out long before I met him: when I had been raped, when kids had beaten me up, when I had sat in solitary, with nothing to keep me company but the grey walls.

Had I forgotten how to cry? Was that possible? In order to survive, I had long since buried my emotions.

Mr. Brawley stopped yelling. Jungle Jim had pulled him away from me. Mr. Brawley turned and walked out of the room without saying another word.

The dorm's house mother took me to the infirmary, where a medic cared for my bleeding nose and badly swollen eye. He told me he would have to take me downtown and have my tooth cared for. The nerve had been exposed, and the pain was intolerable.

At the hospital, a doctor questioned me about what happened. I looked at the floor, refusing to answer him. The medic told him that I had been in a fight with a big kid. The doctor nodded, then proceeded to save my tooth. A discoloration of the lower half of my tooth is a constant reminder of that day.

That night, I ran away from the boys' home. The police spotted me the next morning in Eagle Rock, a short distance from the home.

Mr. Brawley was waiting for me when the police brought me back. He took me into a room next to his office, a room used for board meetings, and whipped me with a razor strap. It was the last time Mr. Brawley was ever to touch me. Compared to the whippings I would receive in other institutions, I realized his were mere love taps.

After the whipping, Mr. Burger called me into his office across the hall. He put his arm around me, and comforted me. I needed that right then, though I would not have admitted it, even to myself.

He held me for a few moments, and I began to feel better. He took me to the kitchen and gave me milk and cookies. He didn't say much, but he didn't have to. He was caring and understanding, and made me feel not everyone was out to get me.

After I finished eating, Mr. Burger told me to stay out of trouble. He said if I was having problems, I was welcome to bring them to him.

During that summer's school vacation, all the kids went to

the home's annual two-week outing at Dana Point. We set up tents and learned how to cook fish and other meals over a camp-fire. I hated the taste of fish and still do, but I liked fishing. I always felt sorry for the fish, though. I threw most of them back in the water.

What I enjoyed most was wandering off by myself, finding sea shells, playing with crabs. All the pressures lifted from me as I sat in the sand, staring at the waves or making small sand castles.

We had been instructed to use the roped-off path while walk-ing down to or coming up from the beach. Camp was set up about 100 feet above the beach. There was a wide path etched in the cliff. It was roped off so we would have something to hold on to as we walked.

One day, I decided to climb up the side of the cliff farther down the beach, to a spot that appeared as if it were a cave's entrance. I was able to reach my goal but found it was not a cave but a shadow.

I have no idea how it happened, but on my way down I lost my footing and fell about 40 feet.

Someone saw me fall and got me the help I badly needed. I had cuts and bruises all over my body. I broke my leg and jaw-bone. I hadn't lost consciousness, but I was losing a lot of blood and felt myself going into shock.

Bringing me up from the beach was extremely difficult. Jungle Jim was there, kneeling on the ground, talking to me until an ambulance arrived. The medics placed me on a stretcher, cov-ered me with a blanket, and we began the long trip up the path to the top of the cliff. I was dropped once and lost consciousness.

I woke inside the ambulance. Jungle Jim was sitting beside me. At the hospital, he told me I was going to be put to sleep. He said when I woke up, I'd be all fixed up. As I was being wheeled into surgery, someone said Mom and Dad had been called and were on their way. They would be at the hospital when I awoke.

Many hours later, I came out of my drug-induced sleep. The first person I saw was Dad standing over the bed, looking down at me. He leaned over and kissed me on my forehead. I tried to speak but couldn't. My jaw had been wired shut.

It was the first time in years that Dad had kissed me, and I remember I wanted to tell him I loved him but wasn't able to. Sadly, I can't recall ever telling him just how much he meant to me.

During my seven weeks at the hospital, Mom and Dad visited often. I was eventually able to make myself understood, though my jaw was wired shut. When I was released from the hospital, I was returned to the home. The wires from my jaw had been removed, but the cast remained on my leg.

Mr. Burger was standing outside, ready to welcome me back. He pushed me in my wheelchair to the infirmary and then to the kitchen.

Over cookies and milk, Mr. Burger told me that Mr. Brawley was thinking of sending me back to juvenile hall. He considered me to be too much of a problem and felt the boys' home was not equipped to handle the kind of trouble I was causing. That frightened me; Mr. Burger must have sensed it.

He pushed me back to his office, where he walked behind the wheelchair and placed an arm over each of my shoulders.

"I think I can convince Mr. Brawley to give you one more chance," he said. "I'm going to help you."

I do not recall all of his soothing words, but I do remember when I suddenly realized his hand was down inside my pajamas, fondling my penis. He continued to assure me he would be able to help me. I sat there, uncomfortable, but not surprised at what he was doing. Something inside me had expected it but had hoped it wouldn't happen.

As uncomfortable as I was, my instinct told me that should I stop him from doing what he was doing, I'd be returned to juvenile hall.

I sat there, not saying a word, not moving. As I had recently reached puberty, Mr. Burger was able to play with my penis until I reached my first climax. It frightened me, although there was a certain amount of physical pleasure.

Mr. Burger pulled his hand away. I felt a wetness and apologized, fearing that I had done something to make him angry. I felt guilty, too, as do most victims of child molestation, who feel that they are somehow responsible for the incident, particularly if the molester inflects pain.

Mr. Burger told me I had done nothing wrong. He said he was glad I had done it, whatever it was I had done.

I put my hand on my penis and felt something strange. I asked Mr. Burger what it was.

"All men do it," he said, unzipping his pants and pulling out his penis. "I'll show you."

He grabbed my hand and put it on his penis. He moved my hand up and down. When I saw him climax, I thought it looked ugly. I felt dirty, and I was frightened.

I look back and realize Mr. Burger was an excellent manipulator of children. Mr. Brawley had probably never intended to return me to juvenile hall. Mr. Burger simply knew it was the right thing to tell me.

Despite the guilt and shame, I began to like Mr. Burger. I felt he really cared for me, that he was the only person who understood me. He always told me he wouldn't let Mr. Brawley send me away. He would often give me a dollar so I could take my girlfriend to the corner drug store and buy her ice cream and soda. I felt he both loved and protected me, and I knew I made him happy when I did those things he wanted me to do. Besides, I figured, he never did anything that hurt me badly, like the other two counselors had done.

Mr. Burger was able to get me alone with him several times each week. We would always do the same thing we had done the first time in his office. A couple times he put his mouth on me and tried to get me to do the same, but I would not do it. He often tried to kiss me, too, but I never let him do that, either.

It all ended one day when he tried to force me to put my mouth on him. He grabbed my hair and pushed me toward him. He frightened me with his roughness, and I began hitting him. I accidentally hit him where he rather would have had my mouth. I ran out of his office. I knew he would look for me at the dorm, so I hid in the equipment room, and stayed there until dinner.

For days afterward, he tried to lure me back into his office. I refused. He had hurt and frightened me. I promised myself not to be alone with him again.

Mr. Burger must have been frightened himself. Surely, he was concerned I would tell someone about what had gone on between us.

But during my stay at juvenile hall, I had learned that a kid does not snitch on others. If he does, he gets hurt. And I had learned there would be no one to tell, even if I had wanted to. The adults didn't care. They found it entertaining to watch kids beat up and molest each other. Molestation was nothing to worry about, they reasoned; it was a "phase" the kids would outgrow.

I graduated with honors from the Optimist Home for Boys. Counselors used the term to assure everyone I had been rehabilitated during my stay and was ready to go home and live peacefully with my family and the rest of society. "With honors" meant that all my problems had been recognized and successfully dealt with. From then on, they assured, I would be a good little boy.

Part of me wanted to leave and part didn't. It seemed a lifetime since I had been home. I had adjusted to life at the boys' home. I was no longer being molested by Mr. Burger or picked on by the other boys. I felt comfortable there and feared what awaited me at home.

I graduated in an evening ceremony. My parents sat across the room, watching the graduating class. We were dressed in blue gowns, and all of us received diplomas. A photographer took pictures. It was an emotional scene as we stood tall, looking down to watch our parents crying happily, knowing that before the evening was over they would be taking their sons home.

Most of the boys, I noticed, were teary-eyed as well. I was not. I couldn't get used to the concept of going home. After a final dinner of steak and potatoes, I said my goodbyes to the staff and to the boys who would remain there at the home.

**The Abbott Family, 1955.**
Dwight, age 13, arrives home from the Optimist Home for Boys
(left to right) Danny, stepsister Carolyn, stepbrother David,
Betty (Dwight's mother), Dwight, Dwight Sr.

# SIX

From the moment of my arrival home, it was apparent that time and circumstance had created an awkward gulf between me and my family. As the weeks passed, it became obvious that gulf would not be bridged.

I was often sullen, angry at things I did not understand. I felt like I did not belong to — or even was from — the same family. The other kids had their own interests, and they did not include me. David was still being an ass, and I avoided him as much as possible. It did not surprise me that Carolyn and Reid made no attempt to make me feel like part of the family.

With my brother Danny, it was different. Before I got in trouble, we had been inseparable. While I was away, he found other things to do. He even had a steady girlfriend, whom he would later marry. There was no room for me. I was hurt, but now I realize that he was not rejecting me, as I had assumed.

I became jealous of Danny and all the things he had accumulated. I was jealous of his girlfriend and male friends.

Danny had a motorbike that he loved and treasured. He did not want others riding it. That included me. I was angry, because I saw his refusal to let me ride it as more evidence that he no longer loved me.

Summer vacation was near, and I was home while Danny and the other kids were at school. One day, I took Danny's motorbike out of the garage and went riding. I had never ridden one before, and it did not take long for me to wreck it. I hit a curb turning a corner. The handlebars bent when I hit the pavement. Much to my dismay, Danny was home by the time I arrived back.

Inside the house, he was very upset. I became defensively angry, not because he was giving me a bad time, but because I knew I was wrong. I felt terrible about wrecking his bike. One word led to another, until I kicked him where a guy doesn't really want to be kicked. He fell down, crying, and I ran out of the house.

By the time I returned home late that night, I decided I didn't want to live there. Though my family had tried to get along with me, I was unable to communicate with them.

Dad enrolled me at Harding Military Academy, in Glendora. I was to attend school 12 hours a day. That assured I would be home only during the evenings.

I didn't last long there. I rebelled. As far as I was concerned, anyone in a position of power was not to be trusted.

The school administrators persuaded Dad to grant the school psychologist permission to interview me. He interviewed me six times over a few weeks. The following is the confidential report he submitted to the academy and to my parents:

> I have had the opportunity to talk "to" Dwight for six sessions, each consisting of two hours. I have purposely emphasized that it was I who talked "to" him, rather than "with" him. From what little he would say during these sessions, and as a result of some testing he agreed to participate in, I find him to be a highly intelligent 13-year-old male who, on the surface, appears to hold an "unreasonable" contempt for authority.
>
> But, when looking a little deeper, and considering what little information he has let slip out, I get the feeling that it is not authority alone that he holds in contempt.
>
> I am certain that we might conclude that it is for all adults that this contempt is directed. Why this is something he feels so deeply, I am able to only hazard a guess. But, I would like it to be clearly understood that my guess is drawn from my 19 years of working with troubled children.
>
> I would say that Dwight, at some time in his life, has been severely abused. I am reasonably certain that the abuse was not from his parents since they are the only people he has indicated any feeling for, other than his brother Danny.

His present disruptive behavior, and refusal to communicate, is but a surface sign of the emotional and mental distress this boy attempts, so very well I might add, to hide.

He has, seemingly, unreasonable fear of adults that he comes into contact with outside of his home. This I am able to state as fact, rather than a guess. I can only regret that Dwight felt unable to trust me so that he could talk about what is bothering him. Since he was unable to, I must draw my conclusions from instinct developed during my years as a child psychologist.

Therefore, I do conclude: Dwight is, or has been, a physically abused child and is now seriously disturbed, emotionally and mentally, as a result. I feel it will be impossible for Dwight to adjust at Harding, and that for the good of the other children, Dwight should be removed from this academy.

Dwight is, obviously, a seriously withdrawn boy and will need considerable therapy and counseling by professional personnel. Should help in this matter not be immediately forthcoming, Dwight will become an even more difficult, if not impossible, child to deal with.

The report was actually a prediction of my future.

My folks removed me from Harding and sent me to a private Christian school. I stayed there a week.

The first day, a male teacher walked up, put his arm around me and told me he loved me. I thought, "Here we go again."

I refused to do what I was told. I threatened to beat up the teachers. I intimidated some of the boys, as I was bigger in muscle than the average kid my age. The schoolmaster made me sit outside his office until classes were over.

I might have made it there if that one teacher hadn't said he loved me. At my age, I had no idea it was the way of a Christian.

I was expelled the day a teacher walked into the boys' bathroom and caught me showing some kids how to masturbate. The strict Christians had no understanding for such things, although I think most kids do circle jerks at some stage of their life.

Dad put me to work in his plating shop and didn't force me to attend another school. He paid me $1 an hour, which was good money for a 14-year-old in those days. My pay averaged $40 a week, and I felt very content. It saved Danny a lot of money, too, since I had a habit of robbing his piggy bank while he was at school.

One weekend, while at the movie theater in town, I met a beautiful girl with golden brown hair. She said her name was Terri, and told me that she lived in a girls' home just a few blocks from my house. The juvenile court had placed her in the home after becoming a problem her divorced mother didn't want to handle.

Terri and I talked throughout the movie. She told me I could visit her on evenings during the week and on days during the weekend. Outside the theater, we said goodbye, and I walked back home with my head in the clouds, unable to think of anything but her. I hadn't socialized with many girls, in or out of institutions. I convinced myself that this was love.

That weekend, I walked over to the girls' home to see Terri. Her friends watched from across the lawn, giggling. I visited Terri almost every evening after that, and I'd always wait out front of the theater when they were allowed to go. This went on for several months.

Terri was 13 and had been through a lot in her short life. Her father had left home when she was 10. Some man raped her two days before her 11th birthday. She hadn't told anyone but me. After running away from home many times, her mother asked the juvenile court to send her to a foster home. There, Terri was one of many young girls molested by the husband of the woman who ran the home.

Terri was very unhappy at the girls' home. She told me she was thinking of running away. I panicked when she said that. I didn't want to lose her. I suggested my parents might allow her to live at our house. I did speak with Mom and Dad, but they told me it wasn't possible.

The next time I saw Terri, I told her she couldn't stay with my family. We talked for a long time then decided the next weekend we'd run away together after I'd received my paycheck.

Saturday night, we met in front of the theater then bought two tickets. Inside, the lights went out, the movie began, and we slipped out to the parking lot. I soon found a car with keys left in the ignition. Within seconds, we were inside the car and on our way to Las Vegas.

We spent that night in the car, parked near Lake Mead. The next morning, we drove to Willow Beach, where I used to give beer to that wild burro. I had an uncle who owned a motel there. I figured he would let us stay in one of the rooms.

Being young and immature, we thought we could fool anyone with a good story. I told my uncle Terri and I had just gotten married and were looking for a place to live and work. The story was a whopper, but he gave us a room, anyway.

The next evening, my uncle told me Dad was on his way to take us back to California. We decided we had to get out of Willow Beach. Later that evening, I climbed through the window of the motel's restaurant and removed the cash left in the register. We jumped into our stolen car and drove off.

A few hours later, while driving through Prescott, Arizona, a police officer spotted the car and arrested us. They sent Terri back to her mother. I was jailed on two federal charges — one for taking a stolen car across a state line, called Dire Act, and another for taking a minor across a state line for immoral purposes. Two weeks later, the police released me to my father's custody.

When I returned home, no one made a fuss about my latest run-in with the law. They tried to talk with me but didn't get too far. I climbed back into my shell. They left me alone.

I made many attempts to contact Terri but couldn't. Her mother forbade her to speak with me. I never learned if Terri was even living at home. After many years, I still feel love for her. I often wondered if she bore our child and what became of the child if she had.

Mom told me years later that Dad felt the only way I was going to get my life together was if he moved the family out into the country. She said he felt if he moved the family, I could get away from the places that held only bad memories for me. And that's the reason we moved to Redding, California.

Although my father's actions indicated how much he tried to help me, they also showed that he had no idea what was happening within me, and why. Although we loved each other very much, we found it impossible to talk. Many times, he asked if there was anything he could do for me or if there was a problem I might want to discuss. His efforts to help were clumsy and futile. He would just nod his head when I shook mine.

In Redding, Danny and I got along better. I still felt guilty about wrecking his motorbike, and found it difficult to approach him. But we went hiking and fishing together, and we did all the things brothers should.

Our new home was surrounded by 40 acres of land. We never ran out of things to do. A small creek ran through the lower end of the property. We swam there and fished for perch. A married couple lived down the road and across a meadow. Danny and I would go to their home whenever we walked to the creek. The woman always had freshly baked peanut butter cookies waiting for us. To eat those cookies, Danny and I did not consider the mile walk any great ordeal. Life was good to the two of us, and our relationship strengthened. But fate dictated those good times would not last long.

Dad still ran his business in the Los Angeles area, and he stayed there for long periods of time. Once a month, he'd travel to Redding and stay for the weekend. Even had he been around when David started bothering me again, I doubt I would have told him anyway.

While incarcerated, I had learned to not tell on anyone, for any reason. The worst act a guy could commit was to snitch on his fellow inmates. I carried that code into the free world and included in it a stepbrother who went out of his way to make my life miserable.

David found the opportunity to slug me one day when Dad was away. Then I lost control. I found Dad's loaded shotgun and went out to the porch to wait for David's arrival. I knew he'd come looking for me. He never knew when to stop bothering me.

When David rounded the corner of the house, he saw the gun and stopped dead in his tracks. Like many other people later in my life, he did not realize the true and real danger he faced.

I raised the shotgun. He showed no fear. Suddenly, from behind me, Mom reached around and grabbed the gun's barrel. To this day, I believe I would have killed David had Mom not intervened. Since that time, I have killed people for doing the same thing David did. He underestimated me.

As Mom took the gun, David lunged for me. She stopped him. Inside the house, I told Mom I was going to kill him. She must have believed me, because she telephoned Dad and described what had happened. She hung up and told me Dad was going to fly up to get me, and take me down to El Monte with him. Meanwhile, Mom took me to a motel for the night.

In the morning, Dad picked me up at the motel. On the way back to the house, he tried to get me to talk to him. He pulled to the side of the road and parked along Highway 44. He insisted I tell him what my problem was. But it was much too late. I had reached a point in my life when I was convinced I had to solve my own problems.

I did tell Dad that if I stayed in Redding, David would have to go. I said nothing else about the matter, even when Dad became visibly angry at my refusal to talk. I wanted to talk, but could not form the words with my mouth. Dad said if I was unable to manage at home, I would be the one to leave.

He didn't mean it, although I thought he had. Later, he told me over and over he hadn't meant to say that. He said he was only trying to shock me into talking with him.

At the house, I stayed outside while he went inside and spoke with Mom and David. Dad came back outside and told me I would be going with him to El Monte, in the morning. I really liked Redding. I didn't want to leave. I asked him why David couldn't leave. Dad said someone had to be at the house to help Mom.

That night, I ran away. I hitched a ride to downtown Redding with a guy who kept putting his hand on my leg while he talked. Every time he'd remove his hand, he put it a little higher up my leg.

At first, I was unsure of his intent. I thought he was just being friendly, although I felt uncomfortable to be touched at all. When I realized what he was doing, I was too frightened to say anything. It was dark, and I began to think of all the things he would do to me if I made him mad.

The fact I had a knack for getting into those types of situations put yet another guilt trip on me. I really felt it was something about me, something I did or said, that made people want to molest me. I was yet to learn that there are many people who seek out kids in my situation. Small, blond, young, cute and alone. As much as I hitchhiked, it is a wonder I had not been raped, killed and buried somewhere.

The man finally got the front of my pants open. When he finished with me, he handed me $5. I asked to be returned to town as he drove me aimlessly through the industrial area. He asked if I'd like to stay with him for awhile. I told him that my parents were waiting for me at home. He stopped the car and let me out. With the money he had given me, I rented the same motel room I had stayed in the night before. As I laid in bed, I wondered what I was going to do.

The next morning, I made up my mind to go to El Monte with Dad. I called home, and Mom told me he had already left. I hung up the phone. There was no way I was going back home. I walked out to the road and stuck out my thumb.

My first ride took me to Bakersfield. The next took me to Los Angeles. Just outside the city, the driver said something I didn't understand. Suddenly, I heard a siren. The man drove faster. It was easy for me to see he had no intention of stopping. Within a mile or so, seven police cars were speeding after us. I looked at the speedometer and saw we were going 100 miles an hour.

The chase lasted five more minutes. It ended when the driver swerved to avoid hitting another car. We rolled several times.

The driver was seriously injured. I received a few cuts and bruises but was not really hurt. I crawled out the window on the passenger's side.

It might appear I was lucky, but a time came when I wish I had died. The car turned out to be stolen, and the police accused me of being involved with the theft. The police told me I would be detained at Los Angeles County Juvenile Hall.

The next day, sitting at a counselor's desk, I learned the driver had said that I picked him up as he was hitchhiking.

"According to the police report, you're a chronic runaway and you stole that car," the counselor said. "You've got a prior record for stealing cars and running off. And this time, you attempted to elude police, causing serious injury to the passenger."

He said the report also stated police had been in contact with my family, who told the police I was incorrigible. My parents had thought there was nothing more they could do with me, he said.

At that moment, I became convinced my parents had given up on me and no longer loved me. Two years later, I learned neither the police nor the juvenile authorities had contacted them. The police report was entirely false. It did not state that I was the passenger and the other person — a much older man — was the driver.

I told the counselor that I hadn't stolen the car and didn't know who had. I told him I hadn't driven the car at all, let alone crash it. I told him I hadn't been running away from home.

In his report, he wrote:

> After talking with Dwight over a period of two days, I feel certain that the child has a great need for psychiatric treatment. He is apparently suffering from hallucinations and is not in touch with the reality of his situation. I am led to be firmly convinced that this child is mentally ill and should be placed in the state hospital for treatment.

The judge accepted the report without question. He ordered me confined to the state mental hospital at Camarillo, near Oxnard. I was to be held for what the judge called "an observation period" of up to three months.

The next day came my introduction to the inhumane institution for the mentally insane.

Camarillo administrators assigned me to ward eight, usually reserved for adult patients. I have no idea why I wasn't placed in the children's ward. I explained my predicament to the ward doctor. He wouldn't respond to anything I said. I became angry, and could no longer speak clearly.

The doctor took that as evidence of my "insanity" and prescribed me little orange and blue pills. Soon, I couldn't walk a straight line, stop drooling, or even think clearly.

I began faking that I swallowed the pills. I hid the pills under my tongue, then spit them in the toilet. In a few days I felt normal again. The ward doctor told me that since I appeared more alert and was obviously no longer hallucinating, the medication must have been effective.

One day, while walking to the chow hall, I made up my mind to escape. I clambered over a building that separated the insane from the sane. I ran my butt off, only to be caught in town by the police. They returned me to the hospital, where I was assigned to an even more secure ward, where the most dangerous of the insane were contained and treated in the most barbaric manner imaginable.

Two doctors immediately gave me a shot that drugged me so badly that I couldn't get out of bed for several days without help; that is, after they unbuckled the leather restraining straps from around me. They kept me straight jacketed for an entire week. The pills began again, and they checked my mouth to ensure I was taking them. Eventually they stopped checking, and, using the toilet, I began to get the fish high in the Santa Barbara Channel.

I began observing the nurses coming out of the medication room. They'd rarely bother to lock the door. Through the crack in the door, I discovered a window in the room. It was the only window on the entire ward that didn't have bars and a heavy screen.

I sat near that room for several days, pretending to be in a drug-induced stupor. The nurses became used to seeing me there and became careless. I got up my nerve one day to stick my hand in the door jamb, keeping it from locking shut. I looked around the ward. No one saw me as I walked into the room and shut the door.

In a flash, I was out the window. I would have gone a lot farther than I did, had some snitch patient not seen me running past another window. He began yelling so loudly that I could hear him outside. They caught me before I made it off the grounds. They gave me another injection and laid me down to rest.

For days, I couldn't think straight. The drugs ran my thoughts all together. It was during that time they had begun experimenting with shock treatments. I was one of the guinea pigs.

Years later, I obtained my medical report:

> It is obvious that this troubled child is psychotic and that medications are not having the desired effect. He is unable to communicate, being in a near-catatonic state of mind. Therefore, it would appear appropriate to recommend a series of ECT [electro-convulsive therapy] treatments, after which the child should again be evaluated.

One morning, a nurse told me not to eat breakfast and to stay in the dorm area with several other patients. After everyone had gone to eat, 12 of us remained. Nurses took us into the hallway and told us to sit on a bench against the wall.

One at a time, those seated nearest a door were led into a room. Moments later, medics wheeled the patient out the door on a gurney. Without exception, each patient appeared very pale, with a black object in his mouth.

To be honest, none of the patients looked too good before going in. Coming out, they were frightening. Most had a trickle of blood leaking from their mouths. Their skin was a pasty color. Their breathing was strange and labored.

When my turn came, I was convinced I wanted no part of whatever was going on in there. I thought they were killing those guys and were preparing to waste me too.

They carried me, kicking and screaming, into the room and laid me on a gurney. They held me down, and I stopped screaming only after they forced a black rubber tube into my mouth. That tube, I learned later, was used so I wouldn't swallow or bite my tongue while they zapped me with electricity.

Looking up at the several male aides who held me fast to the gurney, I felt more frightened than I had ever been before. I saw the doctor adjusting a few dials on a black box. A nurse smeared something on both sides of my forehead and applied a metal disk to each temple. The nurse said, "Ready." The aides grabbed me tighter.

A brief flash like a lightning bolt went across my eyes. My jaw involuntarily bit down on the rubber tube in my mouth.

When I regained a semblance of consciousness, I was standing in line to get something to eat, along with the rest of those who had shared the hellish ordeal. I had a terrible headache and, at first, could not remember what had happened. That whole day passed before I could think clearly and become fully aware of my surroundings.

I realized later that ECT was also used as a form of punishment. Patients who were not on the ECT list but who acted out in any manner to threaten the staff were zapped as soon as a doctor arrived.

One day, sitting on the bench against the wall, I watched them juice a man for several long sessions, who had earlier jumped a nurse. They had accidentally left the door open. Each time they shocked him, his body jerked all over. Foam began to bubble from his mouth, and he made strange noises.

An aide saw me watching and kicked the door shut. I have no idea how many times they zapped that man after the door closed. He was in there a long time.

I underwent the same treatment five times during the next two weeks before I made a successful escape. There is no way of ever knowing the damage those treatments caused me. My inability to recall certain events is likely one result. Several doctors have told me those "treatments" may very well have permanently altered my behavioral pattern for the worse.

I befriended a male orderly who took a liking to me. He spent much of his time talking with me whenever he was working on the ward. He let me know that he did not approve of what was happening to me there. He was always saying that if he and his wife didn't need the money so badly, he would quit his job.

He was present the morning they gave me my fifth shock treatment. The sight had a terrible effect on him. I remember him telling me that my chart said the ECT was having a slow but favorable result in my case. The orderly said it was the doctor and not me who was crazy.

I told the orderly that I had ended up at the hospital because I was trying to get to my father in El Monte. I'm not sure which one of us first mentioned the subject of escape, but he told me that he'd go to the parking lot during his break and leave his car's trunk ajar. Then, when it was dark, after his last dorm check, he would let me out the back door of the ward. I was to go to his car and lock myself inside the trunk. He pointed to his car through a window.

As I waited for him to make his rounds, I was unable to convince myself he was really going to do it. I was so afraid he'd change his mind. But, as it turned out, I was inside the car's trunk when he got off work.

Once he had driven off the hospital grounds, he let me out of the trunk so I could sit in the front seat with him. We didn't talk much during the drive to El Monte, but I still recall his laugh as he described the turmoil that night on the ward, when I was discovered missing and no escape route could be determined.

His concern for me was obvious. I promised him he needn't worry about telling anyone what he had done, even if I was caught. I kept my promise, until now. After all these years, I guess it no longer matters how I escaped. Thank you, my friend.

The orderly who helped me escape dropped me off near Dad's

metal shop. I walked to his house, which was situated in front of the shop. Dad was happy to see me. I told him where I had been and how I got there. He said he had not been contacted by the police or juvenile authorities. I thought he was lying, and was afraid he'd turn me over to the police. I ran off that same evening, only to be picked up by the police a few minutes after I stole a car.

The juvenile court decided I should be committed to the California Youth Authority, at the Fred C. Nelles School for Boys, in Whittier.

Nelles is an institution where children are locked in solitary confinement for months at a time. Physical, sexual and emotional abuse are hidden behind the locked doors, and rationalized to the public as "rehabilitation."

At Nelles, I was introduced to a way of life that was to take my last vestige of love and innocence and tranform it into pure unadulterated hate.

# SEVEN

Driven up the road toward Nelles, I noticed first the high fence that surrounded the entire institution. Along the top of the fence were strands of barbed wire. At the front gate, a man carrying a clipboard exited from a small shack. He wrote something down, looked at me sitting in the back seat, then opened the gate.

They let me out of the car in front of a large, red brick building. They unlocked my handcuffs and walked me up a flight of stairs that led to the building's entrance.

The transporting officers handed my file to a counselor. He took me to another room and told me to strip. I sat naked on a bench for a half hour. Another counselor entered the room and handed me a set of clothing.

"During your stay at Nelles, you'll wear these," he said. "No personal clothes."

I put them on, and he led me to another room. There, I stood with my back to a wall and held a square board to my chest. Printed on the board was my name, my California Youth Authority number and the day's date. Several pictures were taken of me standing at different angles.

One of the counselors asked, "Would you like to call your family?"

I told him no.

Another counselor walked out from his office and told me I had been assigned to live in Wrigley Cottage, which housed Nelles' younger kids.

As it turned out, Wrigley was the strictest place there, outside of solitary confinement. Wrigley was the "marching" cottage; its staff must have all retired from the Army, or else were kicked out of it. They ran that cottage like a military school.

Every day at 5:30 a.m., the lights were turned on. Someone blew a whistle, and we had two minutes to wake up, get out of bed and stand at attention long enough for a counselor to count each kid. Usually, we stood for 10 minutes until the count was completed. We often had to stand longer, since many counselors ran out of fingers and toes and lost track of their count. Then they'd begin all over again.

After the count, we had 20 minutes to dress, make our beds, use the bathroom, brush our teeth, wash ourselves and then sit at attention on the wooden benches lining the wall, in what was called the recreation room. We would sit on the benches until 6:30 a.m., when we were ordered to form four lines and stand at attention. We marched in step to the chow hall. All the children incarcerated at Nelles — unless quartered in the disciplinary barracks — ate their meals there.

The food was decent. But we were not allowed to eat until everyone had their food and was standing at attention. The food was lukewarm by the time grace was said.

We were not allowed to talk from rise and shine until after breakfast. If someone was caught, he would be punished in one of the clever little ways that staff used. Some punishments were not so bad. Others were severe.

After breakfast, we returned to the cottage and stood at attention at the foot of our beds while the counselors held inspection. That consisted of ensuring our beds were properly made — military style — and our footlockers were neat and tidy, as the rules dictated. After inspection, we were allowed to use the bathroom.

At 8:30 a.m., the counselors took us outside and marched us in circles around an asphalt yard area for half an hour. At 9 a.m., we began our daily assigned yard duties, consisting of raking leaves, washing sidewalks and scrubbing windows. At 10:30 a.m., we were marched to the recreation yard, which was nothing more than a flat, dirt-covered area. There were no games nor other recreational activities available to us.

At Nelles, all the kids divided themselves into social groups. Each group had its own bunker, dug by fingers and sticks, where they would go and sit. Those large holes in the ground were our only means of privacy from the Man. At no other time were we able to keep out of his sight. Our yard time became very precious to us.

If a boy had been able to get a visitor to smuggle him in some cigarettes, he would pull one from his wallet — where all contraband was kept — tear it in half, light both halves and pass them around to everyone in the bunker.

It was a game for us to smoke, then hide the cigarette once a counselor smelled smoke. Most counselors thought it a game, too. They knew they were unlikely to catch the vicious criminal who broke the no-smoking rule, so they just went through the motions. I never smoked until I reached Nelles. I started doing it since there was nothing better to do.

At 11:30 a.m., we were marched back to the cottage and, again, told to stand at attention by our beds while another count was made. After that, we washed ourselves before we marched to the chow hall for lunch.

The same rules applied during all meals — stand at attention and absolutely no talking.

After lunch we would have a marching drill for 45 minutes. Then we would attend school until 3 p.m. After school, we were lined into formation and marched around the entire reformatory. A half-hour later, we would return to the cottage and be given five minutes to use the bathroom. Then we would sit again at the benches, until we were counted and taken to the drill field for an hour of marching.

Dinner was at 5 p.m., and at 5:30 p.m., we would return to the recreation yard, climb down into our bunkers and have an hour to amuse ourselves.

There was a lot of homosexual activity inside the bunkers. Most of the children had just reached puberty and were frustrated with their new sexual awareness. The kids did not appear to feel anything wrong with all the sexual contact between them. It went on openly, and the words "faggot" and "queer" were unknown to us. It seemed a natural thing to do, I guess, because we had not been told differently.

At Wrigley Cottage, I can recall no pressure applied to the

physically weaker kids. There was no need for it. Most of the actual contact between the boys consisted of mutual masturbation or looking on curiously as another played with himself. Putting one's hands down the front of another's pants and bringing the other to climax was considered normal. It does not seem to me now that these acts mean a child is homosexual. Most kids go through such a stage, although the longer a child is incarcerated, the greater chance he has of choosing homosexuality as his ultimate sexual preference.

I had a great fear of such contact with my peers, due to my experiences in juvenile hall. But I would watch the others do it, since I was curious. It would be a while before I was willing to participate.

At 6:30 p.m., we would have an hour of close-order drill and then return to the cottage, where 40 children had one hour and fifteen minutes to shower and be in bed.

How well I remember the nights there, with so many muffled sounds, as lonely and homesick kids stuffed their faces in their pillows and cried themselves to sleep.

Every day was the same, except for Sundays. On that day, we were allowed visits from our families. Those who did not have family that visited them — and there were many — could go to church or the bunkers.

My family visited me three times while I was there. I learned later that Dad was emotionally unable to deal with me while I was incarcerated. He could not even bring himself to write to me.

I was soon introduced to Nelles' "disciplinary action barracks" since I had difficulty waking quickly and standing at attention in time for morning count. Each time I failed to do so, the counselor gave me a demerit and ordered me to perform extra chores around the cottage. When I received my fourth demerit in one week, I was automatically taken to where the incorrigibles go.

The disciplinary action barracks had four rooms. One was reserved for the showers. The other rooms were a small dormitory with 15 beds, a counselor's office, and another room where we ate our meals.

When I went through the building's front entrance, I walked past the sleeping area. Between that room and the counselor's office, several other children were seated at attention on wooden benches against the dorm's wall.

A counselor directed me toward the shower room and ordered me to remove all my clothing. He handed me longjohn underwear and a pair of socks. It was all I would be allowed to wear during my entire stay there.

I wish I could remember the name of that counselor. He was one of the most sadistic ones I met during my four years in the California Youth Authority.

Once dressed, he told me, "Go to the dorm and sit at attention on one of the benches."

I turned to follow orders when a blow to the back of my shoulders slammed me against the door frame. Then the counselor grabbed my hair and yanked my head backward.

"You're not double-timing, boy!" he shouted. "As long as you're an inmate here, you'll double-time from one point to another. In other words, run!"

He held a piece of rubber hose to my face. "If you don't learn my rules, boy, you're going to wish you had."

Then he shoved me through the entrance, and I ran to sit on the bench at the spot he pointed to. The counselor walked over and stood in front of me. "Never speak to anyone but a counselor. A counselor will speak first to you. Don't raise your hand to get attention for any reason. Sit at attention and look straight ahead at that black dot there on the wall."

He pointed to the wall across the room. I saw the dot.

"When you're in this room, don't ever take your eyes off that dot," he said.

I looked at that dot then made my second mistake. I looked back at the counselor as he spoke. He grabbed my hair, pulled me to my feet and led me to his office. Inside, he slammed my nose against the wall and ordered me to stand at attention.

He shouted, "You must have a hearing problem, boy. You took your eyes off that dot. I told you not to do that."

My next mistake was to start to explain that I had been trying to pay attention to what he told me. I said three words before he yelled, "You don't have permission to speak!" and hit me across my mouth with the rubber hose.

He forced me to stand at attention and face that wall for over an hour before telling me to return to my seat. When I walked back to the dorm room, I fought to hold back the tears. That was the closest I had come to crying in a while. It wasn't because of the pain; I was getting used to that. It was because I was so confused. What had I done to deserve all this punishment?

The first day's punches were minor compared to what I was to experience during the following two weeks. Discipline barracks had its own rules and manners. They differed considerably from what we were used to in our respective cottages.

At all times, when inside the building and not working or sleeping, we were ordered to sit at attention on the bench and stare at the black dot.

At 5:30 a.m., we were allowed ten minutes to make our beds and use the bathroom. After that, we would go directly to the benches and sit there until breakfast, at 6:15 a.m.

We were rationed half the amount of food we ate in the regular cottages. We were not allowed desserts or other sweet foods, including sugar for our cereal. We had ten minutes to eat. If we didn't finish in that time period, we didn't finish at all. I learned to eat quickly. To this day, I gulp my food when I eat.

At 6:25 a.m., we would be back on the bench. The daytime counselor made a head count. At 6:30 a.m., we were allowed to use the bathroom and brush our teeth. At 6:45 a.m., we went back to the bench, where we sat until 9 a.m.

At that time, the counselor led us to an asphalt area outside, which was enclosed on four sides by buildings. No one was able to look in, and we could not look out. For two hours we were ordered to perform exercises that most healthy young adults could not do for very long.

I was in good shape as a result of my past effort to build my body. The counselor saw I could keep up with his orders, when it was meant for us not to do so. He decided I needed extra attention. He made me do more exercises than the others. When I couldn't go on, he would force me to stand up and hit me across my shoulders with his rubber hose. He also made me double-time around the yard until I could not raise another foot.

In the middle of the yard was what appeared to be a telephone pole, cut in half and buried upright into the ground. During the first few days of my stay, I had no idea what it was there for.

I learned later, when the oldest boy hit a counselor. The man walked up behind him while he was doing pushups and kicked him on the butt. The boy jumped to his feet, yelling, and slugged the counselor in the arm. That called for severe punishment.

The man hit him hard on the face, knocking him to the ground. He kicked the boy several times as the boy tried to crawl away. The counselor kicked more, as the boy curled up in his attempt to protect himself from the blows. Another counselor dragged the kid to the pole and handcuffed his arms around it.

One of the counselors returned from the barracks with a razor strap. The other man unbuttoned the flap on the kid's longjohns, exposing his bare bottom. The man then whipped the boy until he bled. They left him handcuffed to the pole until we finished our exercises in the yard.

When such rebellious acts occurred, we all suffered. We were forced to exercise even more, beyond our endurance, until we dropped and no amount of intimidation could get us going.

At 11 a.m., we would walk back to the bathroom, then sit on the bench until noon. Lunch always consisted of a sandwich and a glass of milk.

At 12:10 p.m., we went back to that hard bench. At 1 p.m., we were assigned cleaning duties inside the barracks. The chores were something we all looked forward to, since it gave us a chance to get off the benches and out from under the Man's stare. If we were careful, we were also able to talk, depending on which direction the counselor was looking.

The best job available was cleaning the shower, since two kids would be assigned to it. The Man rarely checked on them.

He had to remain where he could see the majority of the kids. On counselor at a time supervised us; the other worked in the office and came out only in the event of trouble. That allowed the two kids assigned to the showers to talk freely and to masturbate.

When we were in bed at night, if a kid was caught masturbating, he was ordered to stand naked at the foot of his bed, holding himself. Sometimes, he would be made to stand in that position for hours, much to the counselors' amusement.

At 3 p.m., we were allowed 15 minutes to use the bathroom. At 3:15 p.m., we'd be back on the bench. During that 15-minute period, the second shift of counselors came to work, relieving the first.

At 4 p.m., we were led to the yard and exercised for 50 minutes. From there we marched directly to dinner, then to the bathroom, with 20 minutes to shower. At 5:20 p.m., we'd walk to the bench and sit until 8:50 p.m. At that time, we had 10 minutes to use the bathroom then go to bed. One day had ended.

Every day was the same, and never varied. Each kid had to serve at least 14 days in the disciplinary barracks. If he did something wrong before his time was up, he served additional time. Sometimes, kids served 90 days or more.

It was my third or fourth day when I decided I needed to speak with another kid sitting on the same bench a few feet away. I made the attempt when the counselor walked out of the room into the bathroom. Just as I looked away from the black dot and said hello to the boy, another counselor looked around the corner and saw me.

I braced myself as he walked over and pulled me off the bench by my hair. They had a thing about grabbing hair.

I didn't expect him to hit me with his closed fist on the side of my head. And so I lost control. I made the biggest mistake a boy can make while locked inside an institution. I hit him as hard as I could, right on the nose. He caught a good one: I was very well muscled for a boy my age.

The punch landed perfectly. I knew from the sound and from the flowing blood that I had broken his ugly, stinking nose. He stepped backward a few feet, feeling his nose with his hand. The surprised look on his face gave me a moment of satisfaction. But when he called out for the other counselor, my satisfied feeling changed to one of fear.

What happened then was bound to happen sooner or later. The other kids were so sick of the physical and mental abuse that they went off, and I went with them. Benches were broken, and the windows were shattered from their frames. A boy hit the broken-nosed counselor with a chair. Within seconds, there was a full-scale riot.

The man who was introduced to his own chair was down for the count. The other counselor ran to his office and locked himself inside. He made no attempt to help his partner who, at that moment, was being kicked half to death.

I watched as the counselor in the office picked up the telephone. Then, I helped demolish the barracks. There was no fighting between ourselves. We remained intent on destroying the area where our keepers had put us through hell.

Someone got the idea to take a steel pole off one of the beds and break the window that separated the counselor in his office from us. He was the most hated counselor of all. He had hit, kicked or whipped each one of us.

The man beat with the chair lay forgotten as we all watched the window being smashed. The big kid who'd been whipped at the pole crawled through the frame. I saw the terror on the counselor's face. He dropped the phone and backed into a corner.

What were his thoughts? Was he remembering how he had forced each of us to stand at attention, with our noses pressed against the wall, for hours on end? Did he remember how he would kick us while we were on the ground, unable to do another push-up? How he had handcuffed us to the pole and whipped us until our bottoms bled? Was he wishing now that he had not done those things, as he watched two more boys crawl inside the office, both holding metal bars in their hands?

I have been unable to forget what happened next as the boys rushed toward him. He reached into his pocket, pulled out a large pocket knife, opened it and struck out toward them. I watched the blade go deep inside one boy's chest.

No one moved. The child who had been stabbed screamed once, then fell to the floor. With a look of amazement and confusion, the counselor backed into his corner. A long time passed as we stared down at the child, watching blood flow from between his fingers.

During those moments, I realized our keepers were not the invincible adults they appeared to be. I had watched this one experience fear and even terror as the children, gone mad for a time, rebelled and struck out at him with uncontrollable anger and violence. I saw that we, the boys, had only to stand together to stop the brutality and the abuse inflicted upon us, at least for a few moments.

A loud noise made me turn around. I saw a group of counselors rushing through the front door into the barracks. I looked back to the boy on the floor — no more than 12 years old — and I felt like crying. I was not angry anymore. I only wanted to be the boy I was. I did not belong there. I wanted Mom and Dad. I wanted to feel their arms around me, just like it used to be, loving me and protecting me.

I felt someone touch my shoulder and heard him ask me to walk to the bed area. I turned to do as I was asked, but not before I saw a counselor bend down and tenderly pick up the boy and carry him out a side door. I would never see him again.

Two angry counselors roughly handled the man who had stabbed the boy. They took him outside; I never saw him again, either.

The counselors searched each of us then took us to the administration building. They treated us kindly, asking for our versions as to what had happened. After the interviews, they brought us mattresses and blankets. We slept that night in the hallway of the administration building.

The next day, I was assigned to Greenleaf Cottage, which housed the kids who worked in the kitchen. They were also the oldest boys at Nelles. I had no idea why I was placed there, unless it was because I had refused to say anything about the barracks incident.

I was the only 14-year-old at Greenleaf. All the others were 16 and 17. As my luck went, I was also the smallest boy there. That was to quickly become the cause of a lot of problems. I would be a target for the many bullies there and for those who were into heavy homosexual activities.

I had been there for only a couple of days when I realized I was drawing the attention of some of the black kids. They made it a point to stare me down, causing me to look away first. To them, that was a sign of fear and weakness. Since I didn't walk over and ask what they were looking at, they assumed correctly that I was afraid of them. This allowed them to assume I was weak, an easy mark for whatever they had in mind.

The blacks worked hard at becoming physically imposing, much more so than the white kids. Their appearance intimidated me. Every time that I had been badly beaten up by a kid while incarcerated, he had been black.

Fear is an easy emotion to detect in someone; mine was written all over my face. My age difference put me at great disadvantage, no matter what physical shape I was in. I was faced with a no-win situation. I knew the staring black kids wanted me to be their punk.

They began bumping into me, telling me to watch where I was going. I knew they were testing me, but I didn't have the guts to respond. That let them know just how frightened I was.

One day, while doing my job of cleaning tables in the dining room, two of them approached me.

"Step in the bathroom, boy," one of them said.

I told them there was no way I was going to do anything they told me.

The second boy stepped forward and grabbed my shirt. He put a dinner knife to my neck and said, "Do what you're told."

Cold fear seeped into my gut, and then I got lucky.

A counselor walked into the dining room; he didn't see the knife, but said, "Stop running your mouths and get to work."

The next night, several black boys approached, saying they wanted to talk to me in the shower room. I saw a knife in one of their hands, and it scared the hell out of me. It was beginning to look as though I had no other choice but to fight. I knew that after they beat me, they'd do whatever they wanted to anyway.

Just then, one of the biggest white kids in the cottage walked over, with some of his friends.

"Is there a problem?" he asked.

The black kid with the knife didn't say anything, but he showed what he had in his hand.

The white kid said, "If that's how you want to play, let's do it." He and his friends pulled knives out of their pockets. That was the end of the confrontation, as the blacks had second thoughts about the matter.

I was feeling a little bit better when the guy who had done all the talking turned to me and said, "There's no way I'll let any nigger bugger a cute little white boy like you."

He put his arm around me. I cringed, as I did whenever I was touched, but I allowed him to guide me to the dorm.

There, he wasted no time unbuttoning his pants, saying, "I'm going to look after you, but you're going to have to look after me and my friends."

As he pulled out his penis, I began to feel sick to my stomach. I had no choice, and I knew it. I could either do it with them, or they'd let the black guys have their way with me. I wanted to throw up from the fear and the shame I felt.

When he told me he wanted to have intercourse with me, my fear increased. But this time, my fear was to assist me in saying there was no way I was going to let him stick it in me. He suggested another way, and I let him know I was not about to put my mouth on him, either.

Much to my shame, I did masturbate him and his friends, and allowed them to feel my bottom. The blacks never bothered me again, but I had to masturbate the three white guys every day.

After two weeks of that garbage, I decided I was going to escape. That same evening, as we all walked back from work, I took off running. I ran hard until I reached a high fence. I climbed to the top without any problem but then became tangled in the barbed wire on the top. That's where the counselors caught me.

They took me straight to the disciplinary barracks. My good buddy, the counselor whose nose I broke just before the riot, was there to unlock the door from the inside.

From the beginning, he was to cause me so much pain and misery that I wished I'd kissed him instead of hit him. Within minutes, after the counselors who had walked me there left, he was beating me.

It was obvious he didn't know who had hit him with the chair. He'd say even if I wasn't the one who'd done it, I'd never forget him. He was right. I've never forgotten him, and although I don't remember his name, I'll always remember his face.

He took me to the shower, handcuffed me and slapped me around.

"Now, do something when my back's not turned," he said. Yes, he was a brave one, all right. He seemed to have forgotten he was facing me when I broke his nose, which, in fact, was still bandaged.

I spent my waking hours wishing that counselor was dead. For two weeks, I suffered his brutal abuse. My every body movement caused me pain in areas I didn't know existed, where he had kicked me or hit me.

I tried hard to find the guts to kill him, but I couldn't. I was not a killer. Not yet.

When 14 days had passed, a counselor escorted me back to Greenleaf Cottage. That same night, while raking leaves on the lawn at the side of the cottage, me and a kid named Davis ran off. He and I were having the same sort of problems with the other kids. His were more serious than mine. He was being raped every night. He was older than me and had been in a lot of trouble since he was 8 years old. It was his second stay at Nelles.

We had no trouble getting over the fence. At the top, I threw a blanket across the barbed wire, allowing us to climb over without getting our clothes snagged. I still got a few puncture wounds, but that was no big deal. Mostly, I was afraid someone would notice the missing blanket.

Once over the fence, Davis hot-wired a car, and soon we were driving along the highway. We went North but didn't care which direction we went. We just wanted to put some miles between us and Nelles.

During the next few days, I broke into locked homes for money and food. By the time the police arrested us, we had a car loaded with stolen goods. Included in our booty was a rabbit I had taken. I hadn't liked seeing it in a cage so small it could barely turn around.

We were arrested, taken back to Nelles, sent to solitary and had our butts kicked, all in the same day. I was to receive a big surprise the next day.

The following afternoon, Davis and I were escorted to the administration building. There, we were told we were being transferred to the CYA's El Paso de Robles School for Boys, in Paso Robles, California.

The counselors bound us with leg irons and belly chains. We hobbled to a waiting van and were taken straight to Paso. I never looked back.

# EIGHT

During the ride to Paso, Davis and I talked about what awaited us there. We knew Paso was an institution for older kids, but younger ones were sent there, too, when administrators determined they were too difficult to handle. Paso's security was tighter. There were fewer escapes. Davis was as scared as I was.

We were both placed in solitary, which kids there called "the hole." Administration called it the "confinement building."

As directed, Davis and I entered an empty room and removed our clothes. A counselor told us to face him and raise our hands above our heads. Then he ordered us to lift our genitals, as he, supposedly, sought out any contraband we might have hidden there. Then he ordered each of us to turn around, bend forward and spread our ass. Then we lifted each foot, wiggled our toes, and it was over.

It was a humiliating experience, one I have endured hundreds of times since that day. It is not a necessary procedure. It is simply one to humiliate and degrade an inmate. It's the beginning of a long process used to break a prisoner's spirit.

When Davis and I were bent over, one of the counselors whistled and said, "The guys are sure going to like this one." I wasn't sure which one of us he was referring to. The comment made me angry, but I remained silent. I had already learned that some counselors said off-the-wall things like that, just to get a kid to talk back. Then the counselor would have an excuse to whip ass.

A counselor handed us each underwear, a T-shirt and a blanket, then led us to individual cells. Mine was completely bare. Just a toilet and sink. No bed, no chair, nothing.

The counselor shut the metal door. Suddenly, I felt a great loneliness overcome me. Was it ever going to end? Why didn't Mom and Dad come get me? I became more convinced they did not love me. How could they, letting these things happen to me?

During my first 18 months in the custody of the CYA, I was under the impression that my parents could come and get me anytime they wanted to. It is not difficult to picture the head trip this gave a boy.

In solitary, no child was allowed materials of any kind; no books, not even a comb or a toothbrush. If a boy tried to speak with anyone other than a counselor, or broke any other rule, a day was added to whatever time he had left in the hole. They would never bother to tell us how many days we had to serve to begin with, and so we never knew how many were left.

Having only a blanket to wrap around myself during the day — and that blanket serving as a mattress at night — I caught a cold that developed into pneumonia. A counselor took me to the infirmary, where I recovered quickly.

When the doctor released me, a counselor walked me over to the administration building. I appeared before a committee, comprised of several staff members, who decided where a boy lived and worked while at Paso. They also decided if and when a boy was ready for the parole board's consideration for release back into detention barracks.

Members of that committee said my record from Nelles indicated I had been an unmanageable problem. It was suspected, they said, that I was the main instigator of a riot that had occurred in solitary. They said I had not only assaulted a counselor and had broken his nose, but that I had hit the same counselor on the head with a "blunt instrument."

Most of what they said was far from the truth, but it did not matter. When institutions suspect such things, with or without proof of some kind, those suspicions somehow become facts. An inmate may as well do his worst, because he will suffer for the infraction anyway. And a parole board will use it against a prisoner each time he is considered for release.

When the committee asked me about the riot, I said nothing. What was the use?

They told me they felt it was best for me, and for the institution, if they put me in dorm nine. Troublemakers were "better managed" there, they said.

When I walked inside dorm nine, the door locked behind me. The noise died suddenly, as all 30 kids turned to stare at me.

There were four groups of kids in the dayroom, each seated in their own corner. As I soon learned, each group was called a "clique" or a "tip." The straight clique was the toughest. They lived by the honor code of silence. In other words, "Thou shall not snitch."

In another corner was the semi-straight clique. The members there were considered not as tough as those in the straight clique, but they had proven they would fight and would not snitch on their peers.

Across from them sat the semi-punk clique. They were a group of boys who were weaker physically and were somewhat afraid to fight. Some were under suspicion as to whether or not they snitched on others.

The fourth group was the punk clique. Its members were either snitches or kids who orally copulated others or allowed someone to have intercourse with them. Members of the punk clique were considered the scum of the dorm.

A counselor whose desk sat on a stage-like elevated structure oversaw the entire dayroom. When he saw me enter, he asked me my last name and CYA number. To the Man, we were known only our last names and CYA numbers.

The counselor took me to a clothing room, where I was fitted for my state-issue clothing. A man stenciled my name and number on each article of clothing and gave me a pair of black work shoes. The counselor then showed me my assigned bed and took me back to the dayroom area. On the way there, he briefed me on some of the rules. Any kid caught on or in any bed besides his own would go to the hole. I thought to myself that he need not be concerned about me in regard to such things.

He told me that whenever I was not working, using the bathroom, in the shower or in bed, I was to remain in the dayroom. He pointed at a door, directly at the side of his desk and told me it was the entrance to the bathroom and shower.

Fighting, making loud noises, spitting on the floor and smoking outside the dayroom were all considered rule violations. I had to be fully dressed at all times, unless taking a shower or laying in bed. I was to obey all orders issued by a counselor. There was to be no "sex play," he said. He told me to find a seat and sit down.

I walked out onto the dayroom floor. Again, everyone became quiet and stared at me. I became nervous, which was the purpose of the stares. I learned later that if I had not become so obviously nervous, I would have been approached differently. To those kids, any sign of nervousness was a sign of weakness and fear.

In my case, they were definitely right. Yet I was slowly becoming aware that fear could help me survive. I was beginning to learn that fear was not an emotion to be ashamed of, if it was controlled and used to my advantage.

I was scared. I was 14 years old, and afraid of the older boys. I had a gut feeling that bullies were going to start in on me again.

If a boy gave any sign of being in fear, he was tested immediately. Survival depended solely on how well he hid his normal feelings, his need to reach out, to feel loved and cared for. At Paso, the worst mistake a kid could make was to show a sign of being normal. It remains the same to this day.

Not only was I nervous, but unable to meet the eyes of those who stared at me. That made them think, "Here comes another punk." They moved quickly to make things tough for me. Depending on how I reacted, they would decide which clique I was to sit with.

It was a semi-straight clique member who stood and walked toward me. I had no idea what he intended to do until, unexpectedly, he hit me hard enough to cut me deeply, just above my eyebrow. I discovered the cut when I backed away, put my hand to my forehead and felt blood.

I looked over to the counselor. He was sitting at his desk, watching the game being played out. During my stay at Paso, it occurred every time a new kid was assigned to the dorm; same game, different players.

I looked back to the boy just as he hit me on my mouth. I never again took my eyes off someone who was close enough to hit me.

I went off on that boy. I knew how to fight, and I was in good shape. I saw the look of dismay on his face as I began to place my punches well, the way Jungle Jim had taught me. It was obvious the kid had never boxed. He could not block my fists. A good boxer can take out most street fighters.

Every time the kid swung, I was in another spot, hitting him. The counselor allowed the fight to continue for a few more minutes before he got off his butt and pulled me away from the kid.

Keeping a grip on my arm, the counselor asked the kids, "Where does he sit?"

Another kid walked over to me, and the counselor let go of me. I thought that kid was going to start in on me. When he got close enough, I smashed him. Before I could hit him again, he backed away.

"I don't want to fight," he said. "I want to invite you to sit with me as a member of the straight clique."

He led me to a chair and told me it was mine. Other than me, no one was allowed to sit in it. Still bewildered, I sat down. The counselor handed me a towel to stop the flow of blood. He pulled the cut together with a couple of bandages.

The boys always tried to care for their own wounds. Hospital personnel asked too many questions when a kid went to them. That put heat on the entire dorm, for kids and counselors alike.

Someone offered a cigarette. I took a deep drag, beginning to unwind. It took the better part of that day for me to understand what had happened, and why. I learned I would not have been sucker punched had I not appeared scared. Instead, I would have been verbally challenged to fight, with or without boxing gloves. It would have been my choice.

Most fights were bare fisted. They usually happened on the spur of the moment. Most kids preferred bare fisted fighting. It made for a shorter fight.

I lost count of how many fights I saw that first week. There were dozens. Proving yourself is a way of life in juvenile institutions. Though against the rules, it is condoned by the majority of counselors as an acceptable manner in which kids can settle their differences. It's how boys prove they're men.

The punks were those who would not fight. They were often turned out, forced into oral copulation or anal intercourse. Once a child had snitched — or allowed someone to perform a sexual act on him, with the child in a female role — he was considered a sissy or a snitch, sometimes both. The same rules apply to adult penitentiaries or jails.

Life at Paso was not easy. Most of us had been in constant trouble with the law during our young lives and had worked our way through other institutions before being transferred here. The inmates' average age at Paso was 15 years old, but some kids were 12 to 14. Nearly all of us could tell horrific stories of abuse from the moment we had been confined.

I was assigned a job in the shoe shop and was taught how to make shoes. I also learned to sniff glue. Shoe shop was considered a choice job. I was given the position because several members of the straight clique worked there. They more or less told the counselor in charge, called the "freeman," who they wanted there with them. It was easier on the freeman to cooperate with the kids.

These same kids had a sissy assigned there. He didn't just work on shoes. This particular boy was considered the cutest at Paso. He was 13 and very frightened of physical violence. So, he was turned out.

Boys were usually turned out by a member of the straight or semi-straight cliques. In return for sexual favors, the sissy was given protection.

I was still not into sex with anyone, and I had the feeling some of the other guys weren't either. But they committed sexual acts on the sissy to prove they were one of the guys.

I felt sorry for the sissy, but I wouldn't have told anyone that. You never did or said anything that could jeopardize your position. Incarcerated life is like walking on eggs.

As the days passed, I became aware that some of my partners wondered why I wasn't taking the sissy into the bathroom. I began to feel it would not be long before someone asked me if I had a problem. If I said sex with a boy was not my bag, it would be considered an unacceptable response. After all, I was a member of the straight clique, was working in the shoe shop, and everybody there was doing it to that kid.

After our five-hour stints at work, we sat with our cliques, acting tough. A cigarette would hang from the corners of our mouths, and our hands were down the front of our pants. We played with ourselves as if to assure everyone that our hands were not down someone else's pants. We were a bunch of clones.

My biggest fears materialized one day when I was sitting in the dayroom. A new kid arrived from Nelles. His name was Blinky. He was from Greenleaf Cottage, where I had been forced to masturbate the three white guys. I had always dreaded that my past would come back to haunt me.

Blinky didn't notice me when he first walked into the dorm. He was quickly put to the test and was beaten so badly that he was told to sit with the semi-punk clique. An hour or two later, I watched Blinky as he asked for permission to speak with Robert, the president of the straight clique. My gut told me what he was going to say; it was his bid to be accepted by the straights. He was doomed to fail.

Later, someone let me know that Blinky had told Robert that I had been a sissy at Nelles. I could have denied Blinky's story, and that would have been it for the moment. But I knew there would be another episode when someone would come around with the same tale, and I would have to face up to it. So I told the guys what had happened. I told them I had never orally copulated anyone, nor had I allowed anyone to put himself inside me.

As I told my story, I observed expressions of disapproval. They found it difficult to accept what I said. I understood why. That I had done anything at all was a definite sign that I had been scared and weak. It was too much to ask my fellow clique members to understand I would have had to fight three guys, each twice my size. I mentioned the fact that I had not snitched on those three, but that comment was not given any open consideration. All I had going for me at the moment was that they liked me. That was all.

The matter was resolved in an unusual way; I was not immediately told to sit with the punk clique. Instead, Robert and I agreed that we would go to the dorm area by ourselves and fight. My status would depend on how he felt about my fighting ability, my guts and how much heart I showed.

Robert was the biggest and toughest kid in the dorm. He was nearly three years older than me and about 50 pounds heavier. I realized I was in for one heck of a whipping, but that did not concern me as much as the thought of me sitting with the punk clique. I had a choice, and I made it without difficulty. I chose to fight.

Whenever a fight occurred between two members of the straight clique, it was always done away from everyone's sight. Straights fighting straights was never to be for the amusement of others in the dorm. The fights continued until one or both could not go on. Even the counselors accepted this code of honor, because the straight clique kept life on the ward running smoothly, making the counselors' jobs easier.

Robert and I went to the dorm area and closed the door behind us. We removed our shirts, preparing to do battle. Fear crept inside me, but I welcomed it. I embraced it as a friend who had come to protect me from harm, to help me survive.

With no words spoken, Robert rushed me. As he reached out to grab hold of me, I stepped aside and hit him hard behind his ear as he went past. He slammed into the wall, turned, and set himself again. The punch may not have hurt him, but I could tell he wasn't too happy about it, either.

Robert was a street fighter, not a boxer. Had I not been able to avoid half the punches he threw, he might have really hurt me. Each time he swung and missed, I tagged him. That frustrated him, and the anger that came from his frustration made him fight worse than he could have. Jungle Jim had told me many times, "Never go into a fight angry. Never get angry while fighting. Get your opponent mad, and you'll have half the battle won." Boy, was Robert mad.

The fight lasted 10 minutes, at the most. When we called it quits, both my eyes were swollen shut. My nose and mouth were bleeding like a faucet.

Robert looked only a little better. I had broken his nose, and the next day he was to awaken with two beautiful shiners.

We stood several feet apart, gasping. I tried to gauge what he was thinking. So much depended on how he felt. I liked him before we squared off, and I liked him after. I understood what our code had called for and what Robert had had to do. He could have banished me from the straight clique, but instead he had done me a favor by fighting with me.

I stepped back and leaned against a wall. Robert sat down on the edge of a bed. I walked over and held out my hand, but he made no move to grasp it. I said, "Robert, I'm no sissy, and I can't be made into one."

He smiled, stood, then accepted my handshake. He said nothing as we put our shirts on and walked into the dayroom. Everyone was straining to see the result of the fight. They were quiet, wondering what would happen next.

We cleaned ourselves in the bathroom then walked back into the dayroom and went to our seats. I stood next to my chair as Robert sat in his. I watched him, waiting for him to decide what would be done. No one said anything.

As I stood there, I knew that Robert would have to decide if I would remain in the clique. I reached down and picked up a pack of cigarettes. I pulled out a smoke and put it between my lips, all the while willing myself not to shake.

Robert set down the towel he had been holding to his nose. He walked to me, took the matches I held in my hand, then lit the cigarette for me. I was to retain my position and status.

That was the first time I felt total acceptance from my peers. I never again needed to fear my past. It had caught up with me, and I had faced it in a manner that had been accepted.

But the incident was not over. I knew, as did my peers, that I had to deal with Blinky. He had tried to destroy my position to better his own. Had he succeeded, the entire matter would have been finished. But he failed, and our code of honor dictated that I get back at him for trying to do me in.

The next morning I could barely see. One eye closed tight,

and my other eyelid was barely open. My body felt like an elephant had stepped on it. A few days would pass before I would feel anywhere close to normal.

But first I needed to take care of Blinky. I felt no personal need for revenge. I would have preferred for the matter to end, but the code of honor dictated what a kid was to do, despite what he might feel.

I made my move that evening, after dinner. Everyone was relaxing, enjoying a smoke. I walked over to Blinky, standing a couple of feet from him. As he started to get up, I kicked him in the face so hard that the blow lifted him off his feet and knocked him backward over his chair.

When a boy from either of the lower cliques tries to discredit a member of the two top cliques, he is dealt with in a severe manner, and is made an example for all the others. They soon understand that under no circumstances do they mess with a member of the straight clique, unless they can back it up.

I took no chances with Blinky making me look bad. I had to assure everyone who looked at him afterward that they better not mess with me. I vaulted over the chair and landed on Blinky. I kicked him several times in his face. When I realized he was crying, I backed away.

As I looked down at him, I remember feeling like crying along with him. I felt no pride in what I had done. It was just business that had to be taken care of.

Blinky did himself a great injustice by crying. He was instantly demoted to punk status. From that day on, wherever he might have gone within the juvenile or adult penal system, he would have to seek protective custody, which was just another name for solitary confinement.

In my peers' minds, I had proven myself. Unless I went against our code, I would always be a member of the straight clique.

Soon after, I found myself in another awkward situation.

One day, my partners and I were at the shoe shop, sniffing glue. I am sure I was high enough to float over the fence. I walked to the bathroom and, as I entered, I saw two of the guys having sex with the sissy. I turned to leave, but one of them said, "Stay and get your issue."

I wasn't interested. My past was still haunting me. "I don't really feel up to it," I said.

They looked at me strangely, like they were thinking Blinky had been right. That made me angry. It frightened me they would think that. I knew if any doubt was verbalized by one of my clique buddies, I'd have to prove myself all over again

Being wasted from sniffing glue made it easier for me to make my decision. I stayed in the bathroom and got my issue. I felt all empty inside. Getting along with my peers meant that I would never be my own person.

In later years, this influenced me deeply, and I decided to become a loner and take on all people who tried to push me into something I didn't want to do.

When I was finished with the sissy, I realized that I enjoyed it. Later, I would catch myself looking at the sissy, getting aroused. All this created intense emotional turmoil. This was compounded by my not wanting to ridicule the boy, as was expected of me.

The code told us that we must feel and display nothing but contempt for all sissies. They existed only to be used, abused and discarded, without regard to their feelings. I was swept up in this way of thinking. I believed it, and I lived it. It was the way things had to be in order to survive.

I began to make the sissy's life miserable. I forced him to make my bed every morning, to shine my shoes, to light my cigarettes and to get any item I might need or want. All the while I felt ashamed and sorry for him. And he continued to arouse me.

I had numerous private encounters with this boy, and in my own way I tried to show him that I cared about him. Bobby, if you're reading this, I'm sorry about a lot of things.

On Oct. 2, 1957, two days before my 15th birthday, my stay at Paso was to end.

Blinky tried to stab me with a fork. He had smuggled it out of the mess hall — no great feat.

I had been bending over the bathroom sink, washing my face after dinner, when someone bumped hard against me. I turned and saw Robert and another boy holding Blinky. A fork dropped from Blinky's hand and clattered on the floor. I bent down, grabbed it and stuffed it down the front of my pants. I didn't want a counselor to see it. Had the Man seen Blinky try to stab me, we all would have been thrown into the hole.

I looked at Blinky and told him to get out of the bathroom. He would have stabbed me if Robert had not seen him make his move. Sadly, Robert was stabbed to death during a gang fight just 16 months after this incident.

The butterflies fluttered in my stomach. I had almost been stabbed, possibly killed. It was the first time I had actually been attacked with a weapon. At Nelles, when the black boy held a knife against my throat, it was a threat, not a sincere effort to cause me physical harm.

There was never a doubt I had to retaliate. I had to save face. My honor and ability had been questioned. A punk had made an unusual attempt to hurt a straight. No mild retaliation would save face for me or my clique. I had to cut Blinky.

While I worked, thinking about it, I began to feel sick. My stomach always tells me when a rumble is pending.

After lunch, I returned to work. I psyched myself up to feel the anger that would help calm my fear. When the shop's foreman wasn't looking, I slipped a knife used for cutting leather into the waistband of my pants. Robert, always observant, saw me do it. He told me the best time to do whatever I had in mind was when we returned from dinner, when the counselor would be going in and out of the shower room to discourage any homosexual activity.

When I returned to the dorm, I stuffed the knife down the crease of my chair, where the backrest met the cushion. While we sat waiting for our turn to shower, everyone in the straight clique knew what was about to happen. No one else was aware of it. I glanced several times to where Blinky sat, across the room with his back to me. He appeared at ease, probably thinking that nothing would happen during the shower period.

The first two times the counselor checked the shower, I remained seated, building up courage. When for the third time the counselor left his chair, I moved toward Blinky before the counselor was through the shower room door. I stopped behind Blinky. He didn't know I was there. The counselor must have sensed something was wrong. It was too late. The Man had seen the knife in my hand.

"No!" he shouted.

I grabbed Blinky's hair and then brought my other hand down to slice his throat.

His warm blood spurted over my hand and arm. I sensed, rather than heard, the kids in the punk clique screaming. I let go of Blinky and backed away. Some boys ran from the area. It looked like they were moving in slow motion.

The counselor ran toward me. His lips moved, but I heard nothing he said. From the corner of my eye, I watched Blinky stand, turn and face me with an expression that is difficult to describe. He put his hand to his neck. Seeing the blood, his look turned to terror. He fell to the floor and looked up at me, as if to ask, "Why?"

I am not sure if I yelled out what I was thinking, that it was his fault for being such a fool. I think I did. I was more angry at him for having caused the confrontation than trying to stab me. I returned from my dream state.

"Drop the knife!" the counselor yelled.

All the kids were standing against the walls. I searched ·for Robert. In his face I saw respect, an awe for me that had not been there before. Behind that, I saw fear. He realized I had entered another level of violence and brutality.

I smelled his fear, and a door inside my brain opened. Knowledge poured forth and overcame me in waves. We fought to hide our fear, to maintain our positions as predators rather than victims. In reality, we were all victims.

I saw a bunch of kids who needed love and acceptance and to be allowed to live as normal children, instead of having to fight to conceal their misery, fear and weakness.

Several counselors and a nurse ran inside the front door of the dorm. They stopped short when the counselor yelled that I had a knife. The nurse dragged Blinky away from me.

I started walking toward the counselors, holding the knife out from my side. If one of them had reached out to take the knife, instead of backing away, they could have had it. I saw the door they had left open in their haste to get inside the dorm. Because they moved to the side of the room, it was easy to reach the door.

I ran into the night. When I reached the fence, I threw the knife to the ground. I climbed up and over, then ran across the fields that separated me from the hills a mile away.

I was halfway to the hills when I realized I wouldn't make it without resting. I laid down in the tall weeds, hidden from sight, gasping for breath.

I began to run again when suddenly a car's headlights shined on me. I fell to the ground and crawled away from the area where I'd been spotted. I crawled for nearly an hour before I was spotted again.

I ran, and the driver of the car tried to run me over. Finally, I stopped.

Three counselors leaped from the car and yelled for me to put my hands in the air. I did as I was told. They handcuffed my hands behind my back and dragged me to the car. One of them slammed my face on the frame of the open door. The edge of the frame ripped through my cheek and knocked out a tooth. Then they started to beat me into unconsciousness.

I woke inside the infirmary. It was Oct. 4. Happy 15th Birthday. The counselors had left a few presents for me. The night before they had busted my arm and ankle. My cheek is still scarred. I wonder if they were trying to tell me something?

# NINE

As unbelievable as it may seem, two counselors wanted to remove me from my infirmary cell the next day. A doctor protested in vain. Within the walls of all institutions, rarely can a doctor influence administrators to protect a prisoner's health.

The counselors picked me up off the bed and placed me in a wheelchair. They wheeled me to a van, laid me on the back seat and drove me to the Preston School of Industry, in Ione, near Stockton. Preston is where the California Youth Authority incarcerates its most hardened wards.

In truth, Preston was no more than a warehouse for boys who had grown up with abuse instead of love. The staff was unable, or just did not care to realize, that most of us were frightened kids thrown into an alien environment, forced to act in a way that would improve our odds of surviving.

Preston was considerably larger than Paso. When I was there, it housed about 200 boys, who lived in six dorms and what appeared to be a castle. The castle was the first stop for every arrival at Preston, and for every boy it was a horrifying experience.

All the buildings at Preston were surrounded by two fences, with about 30 feet of real estate separating one fence from the other. Huge rolls of barbed wire were strung across the top to remind us that we were vicious, anti-social, unmanageable boys.

Most were there, however, for non-violent crimes like burglary and auto theft. Many were there just for not being able to get along at home or at the other juvenile institutions. Preston was the last stop; we were considered hopeless, no longer reformable.

The kids who ran away from other institutions before being sent to Preston usually headed for the one place they felt they could receive the love and understanding they craved — home. The Man always looked there first.

The standard administrative response to parents' questions was, "Your child has shown a complete disregard for the laws of the state and a total unwillingness to follow rules that would bring about his rehabilitation. Therefore, he has been placed in this school, where he will have a better chance to improve his attitude about himself and others, and learn that he must be a responsible individual. Now he will be closely supervised in an institution that is more secure and able to care for his particular problems."

That is what my parents heard. They believed it for a long time, too.

I must agree it sounds good. It sounds even better coming from a seemingly polite and understanding fellow in a suit. College degrees plaster his wall. He reassures you that he's been working with children for over 20 years. He promises you a "totally different child" in a few short months. He's right on that score. The child will be different.

I spent my first six weeks inside the infirmary, which was the best place to live at Preston.

After being discharged, I was admitted to "A" dorm, where every new arrival was assigned. There, supposedly, the counselors would observe us closely. We would receive "psychological pro-file testing" and be interviewed by several staff members. Then the administration determined which dorm best suited the child's (i.e., Preston's) needs. The assigning process was of much concern to the kids because no one wanted to be placed in the tough dorms.

I tried to remain on my best behavior, but my reputation had preceded me. When I first arrived at A dorm, the counselors told me they were fully aware of what I had done at Paso. They said I'd find myself in solitary if I so much as looked wrong at them or any of the kids inside the dorm. There was no chance for me to begin anew and attempt to show the staff that I was not a terrible boy who had to be watched and feared.

The staff at Paso claimed I had been able to escape because I ran at them with the knife in my hand. They said I had forced them to move away from the door in fear of their lives.

Once a staff member has written something in your file, it is never questioned. The information will be used against you for as long as you are confined.

The reputation I had built at Paso was similar to that of a Western gunfighter. A man considered fast with the draw was sought out by others who wanted to prove they were even faster.

I was not nearly as big as many of the other boys. I had always been small in comparison. The fact I was also considered pretty caused me even more problems than my small size. At Preston, I was to become convinced that every kid in there walked around in a constant state of sexual arousal, looking for easy prey.

My looks and size were deceiving to those who sought to build a reputation by trying to kick my ass. In my heart, I was a kid with no desire for trouble. I felt fear in my gut when I was supposed to fight an older guy twice my size.

I began thinking less about Mom and Dad and about home. During my first two years being locked up, I spent hours each day missing them. They did not visit me often and, slowly, even their looks faded from memory. I became consumed with my own struggle to survive.

My first fight at Preston occurred in the sleeping area. I was lucky it happened there, since no counselors were around to toss me into solitary for breaking the rules.

At Preston, the fights were "anything goes." It made no difference how you won, just as long as you won. That was the main reason we spent so much time making sure no one sneaked up behind us.

Most of the fights took place at night. Once the counselor had made his nightly count, he would leave the bed area and lock the door behind him. The counselors working the night shift left the buildings and returned only for an occasional security check.

I woke to a rain of fists. I was hit several times while working my way out from beneath my sheets and blankets. Luck was with me. The kid doing the punching was not a hard hitter, nor did he know how to fight once we got into it. Had he been one of the bigger and more experienced kids, I may not have been able to make it out of the bed before I was really hurt.

I was left with no choice but to show that I did not appreciate being wakened in such a rude manner. I beat that kid until he laid on the floor and covered his face to protect himself.

Had he been one of those guys who expected everyone to kneel down and kiss his feet, I would have kicked his face until my foot broke. This boy was the kind of would-be bully who was probably suckered into jumping me. It was a way for the bigger bullies to learn how well or how poorly another boy fought.

I backed away and sat on my bed, no worse for wear but out of breath. I looked down at the young boy, not knowing that he was to become my best friend and would soon save my life.

You could see the next day that the kid's face was a mess. To the counselors coming on duty in the morning, such sights were common. When a boy stated he had fallen out of bed, the counselors always shrugged it off.

There were no cliques to speak of in A dorm. They came once a boy was assigned to his permanent dorm. In the meantime, most kids picked a buddy or two and ran with them as a security blanket.

Until then, I had remained alone, apart from the games, hoping I could prevent my placement in one of the hardcore dorms. The fight caused me to begin looking for a buddy who would watch my back. I spent a couple of restless nights while I searched. My heart wasn't into it. I preferred to remain alone.

I needed someone who didn't have a friend and who was neither a punk or a snitch. A couple of the so-called tough guys approached me in an attempt to draw me into their little group, but I made it clear I wanted to pick my own friends.

Of all the kids I watched and considered, only one carried himself in a manner of which I approved. It was the kid who had jumped me. His name was Donald Stubblefield.

He was usually by himself, doing his own time. He seemed to get along fairly well with most of the others. I noticed a couple of the older boys known for turning out punks approached him. But they always walked away, looking mad, while Donald appeared concerned and upset.

At 14 years old, Donald was considered one of A dorm's prettiest boys. He had light brown hair, blue eyes and was small for his age. If the older, bigger boys had succeeded in making him a punk, I would have known about it because I would have seen it happening in the sleeping area.

I sat down next to him in mess hall. He looked at me, in surprise and apprehension. The thought must have crossed his mind that I was there to take up where I had left off three days before. But he hid his fear well, and I liked that.

I finished eating, turned to him and asked, "How do you feel about the fight we had?"

He looked at me, confused, wondering what I was up to. "I've got no hard feelings," he said. He told me he'd been duped into doing what he did, as I'd expected.

Leaving the mess hall, we continued to talk. We spent the entire evening together, allowing ourselves to learn more about the other. I liked him, and I knew he liked me, too, because he let me see a little of what was behind his wall, the wall we each built to hide ourselves behind. Letting those walls down was very risky and could have placed us in danger. By the end of the evening, I had given him the nickname "Stubby."

It was in A dorm that I began to sharpen my senses to a very fine edge. I taught myself to sleep soundly, yet awaken totally alert if anyone came within a few feet of my bed. I could sense stares while my back was turned. And I learned never to sleep with my bedding tucked in. I gave the boy who slept in the bed next to me a package of cigarettes to change beds with Stubby. He and I remained apart from the others and the games they played. By the manner in which we carried ourselves, everyone knew we were not looking for trouble but didn't intend to allow anyone to cause us any, either.

The bullies who had been messing with Stubby no longer said anything to him. Stubby told me he had been afraid they were going to gang up on him and rape him if he did not willingly accept their advances.

After spending nearly six weeks in A dorm, a counselor told me I would soon appear before the classification committee. Stubby had been in Preston nearly two months and thought he should have been seen by classification weeks before. He learned he was appearing, too.

We wanted to be assigned to the same dorm, but we knew no one is given a choice in the matter. We began to feel a bit depressed, because the odds were slim that we would be assigned to the same living quarters.

I faced the classification committee right after Stubby. All they wanted to talk about was the final incident at Paso. They were very unhappy about that. They did tell me it was "noted" that I had been doing very well since my arrival at Preston. They said they had been getting good reports about my behavior. I began to think I would be placed into one of the better dorms.

Then they dropped their bomb. They told me I was assigned to "F" dorm, the worst there. I asked them why. They told me that the institution's psychiatrist wrote that I was "an obvious manipulator" when I expressed my desire to be assigned to one of the honor dorms.

The shrink wrote that he considered me one of the most dangerous 15-year-old boys he had interviewed during his employment with the CYA. He based that judgment upon what he had read in my file and comments I had made to him. He wrote that I "hid from the untrained eye behind a well constructed wall of deception."

I did not fully understand those words when they were read to me, but I got the drift. I became angry, which further convinced the committee members that I was indeed incorrigible.

I had spoken openly and honestly with the psychiatrist for a full 15 minutes, hoping he would see that the events at Paso were precipitated by fear and peer pressure. I tried to convince the shrink that I now knew how to hold steady under pressure, rather than blindly do what others around me thought I should do.

I was not lying to him. I felt I could lay low at Preston and soon be granted parole. I wanted to go home, and the only way I could do that was to stay out of trouble.

All this fell on deaf ears. The committee stuck to their decision to pack me out to F dorm.

I flew off the handle. I told them to shove the shrink's report where the sun don't shine. I got up from my chair to walk out of the room but was ordered to sit back down. The committee members then told me Stubby had asked that we be placed in the same dorm. They said when they told him I would likely go to F dorm and he was to go to the honor dorm, he asked that he be allowed to go wherever I went.

At that moment, I thought Stubby was a fool.

Through my fog of anger, I heard one of them say it was "well documented" that Stubby and I appeared to be a positive influence upon one another. My ears perked up. Maybe they'd send both of us to the honor dorm after all.

I was about to thank them for giving me a chance when I heard, "Therefore, we have decided to place both of you in F dorm. It is our hope that the two of you will continue to exhibit that positive influence over one another and will work your way to an honor dorm and, eventually, parole."

I was mad at Stubby for his loyalty. F dorm was no place for him. Stubby was one of the youngest, smallest and cutest boys at Preston. Sending him to F dorm was like putting a chicken inside a cage with a wild dog. The situation had me panicked. I had my doubts whether I could handle my own problems, much less his, too. Protecting Stubby was not something I looked forward to.

Stubby became disturbed when I angrily asked him what the hell he thought he was doing. I yelled, calling Stubby a stupid son of a bitch. Hurt came to his face. Wetness appeared at the corners of his eyes. I felt bad. The thought nagged at me that Stubby knew I would look after him. I knew he thought I would stand up for him, since he didn't know how to fight.

As we talked, a counselor called our names. "Pack your gear," he shouted. "You're going to F dorm."

The Castle, Preston School of Industry

# TEN

The F dorm sat atop a low hill, near three other dorms. All had been recently built, so the wards could be moved once and for all from the castle, which had been built in 1894. The castle had finally been declared unsafe and unfit for habitation.

Walking into F dorm was like walking into a Paso dorm all over again. The floor plans were identical. The cliques were sitting in their individual corners, and the counselor's desk sat upon its platform. When Stubby and I entered the dorm, I sensed a tension that hung like a cloud over the room.

All the boys turned to look at the two new kids. A few whistled and hooted obscene remarks. They sneered and laughed. Immediately, I felt threatened. It was obvious these boys played more seriously than they did at Paso.

An older kid who looked like he'd pumped iron since leaving his mother's womb approached us.

"I'm the captain of the dorm," he said, pointing to a set of bars pinned to his shirt lapel. "I give the orders. Anyone that bucks me will get his ass kicked."

I believed him.

The counselor showed us to our beds. Then he gave us a tour of the entire building. He told us the rules. They were the same ones I'd heard before. The counselor ordered us to go back to the dayroom and find out where we would sit. The game began.

Stubby walked out onto the dayroom floor with me. He pointed to a chair that wasn't occupied and headed toward it. I grabbed his arm and told him we'd stand against the wall for a while.

As we stood there, holding the wall up, I kept my eyes on the others while I explained to Stubby that we had to wait until seats were offered. I told Stubby we'd be approached, then we would play it from there. I told him he should let me do the talking,

unless someone asked him a direct question, and to start swinging and not stop if anyone did or said anything out of line. He
looked at me, startled.

I stood there, the butterflies doing laps in my gut. I met every
stare without averting my eyes. In that crowd of about 40 kids, I
saw some mighty big ones. A few looked like they'd blend right
in with the crowd at San Quentin. I watched a member of what I
thought was the straight clique walk over to another clique. They
spoke for a bit, then the guy went back to his seat. There was not
much doubt as to who or what was the topic of discussion.

Two other boys stood up, and I was surprised that the possi-
bility of fair play existed. Both boys were about our size. I
watched them walk toward us. In my mind, I chose the fighter of
the two. I told Stubby to punch the guy on the left, on his mouth,
as soon as he was close enough to hit.

"Keep swinging until someone stops you," I said. Stubby gave
me a nervous glance.

That was all the time we had. The kid I'd chosen stepped
closer, and I hit him with everything I had. I could see from the
expression on his face as he looked up at me from the floor that
my fist was the last thing he had expected.

He was out of it, and that gave me a chance to see what
Stubby was up to. He was getting his butt kicked. Somehow, he
had ended up sitting in a chair as his opponent stood over him,
relentlessly punching him in the face. I didn't stop to think if I'd
be out of line to jump in. I just did it. I pulled the guy around and,
before he could set himself, I kicked him into high soprano. He
went down, holding onto his genitals, as if to assure himself he
was still a boy.

Then I was jumped from behind. So much for sharpened senses. Three of them were on me. I don't remember much more than
that.

When I came out of my daze and recalled where I was, all I
could think about was the hurt. I was unable to move my fingers.
Later, I learned three of them had been broken.

I stood up and put my back against a wall so I wouldn't fall
down. I was wondering if the three of them would come back for

seconds. I was trying to locate Stubby, but blood blurred my vision.

I felt someone grab my left arm. I was startled. I turned and punched out with what little energy I had left. I missed. I hit the wall instead, breaking the little finger and a knuckle on my right hand.

"Are you okay?" It was Stubby.

That question seemed so ridiculous that I burst out laughing. Some of the other kids began to laugh, too, and I sensed from the tone that they were laughing with me, not at me.

The dorm captain told Stubby to get me to the bathroom and clean me up. I asked Stubby to get me to a shower. He got my clothes off and turned the water on. The blood washed from my eye, and the cold water slowed the bleeding. I could see from one eye, but the other remained closed as tight as a frog's butt.

The pain began to creep up on me and into my broken hands. The counselor came in to look me over. The swelling around my hands was considerable and colored like a rainbow. He uttered a few choice words, then told me he'd have a van take me to the infirmary.

I squinted at myself in the mirror. The cut over my eye was gaping so wide that a flap of skin hung down, resting on my eyelid. The swelling around my closed eye was about the size of a baseball. I looked down at my hands, and what I saw made them hurt even worse. They did not look like hands, just round objects I was unable to move. I consoled myself thinking that I need not worry anymore about being a pretty boy.

Stubby's only apparent injury was a black eye. A slight trickle of blood leaked from one of his nostrils. I felt good that he was all right. His obvious concern for me was touching, and I assured him that I would live, even if I didn't feel like it for awhile.

Someone shouted that the van was ready. Since the infirmary didn't have a regular doctor on duty and was not equipped to treat major injuries, I was soon on my way to a hospital in town.

When I was admitted, a doctor asked me to describe what happened. He didn't seem to believe me when I said I'd slipped in the shower. A nurse standing nearby said, "It seems like a lot of you boys fall down in there."

After I came out of surgery, the doctor told me he had repaired six fractures in my hands. It had taken 17 sutures to close the cut above my eye. I had cheekbone fractures, too, which the doctor assured me would heal without treatment, "as long as you don't slip again in the shower."

I stayed at the hospital that night and returned to Preston the following day, with a fresh cast on each arm. Some administrators questioned me about the accident, and I was returned to F dorm after refusing to go to the infirmary. I was worried about Stubby.

The first thing I saw when I walked into the dayroom was Stubby sitting with the punk clique. I told him to stand up. We walked over to the wall together.

"No way you're sitting with those punks," I told him.

"But I had no choice. They were..."

"We always got a choice," I said. "Even if we got to kill someone."

Stubby looked at me as if I was nuts. Maybe I was. I knew who was who, and I stared at the three guys who had creeped up on me. Stubby had told me they were all members of the straight clique.

What noise there had been, ceased. The dayroom was so quiet, all I heard was my heart beating in my chest.

Only one of the three stood. He came over and stopped just out of range. His name was Carl. He and I both knew I'd use my casts to beat his head in.

"I didn't come to fight," he said. "I came to tell you you broke the rules when you jumped the guy who beat your friend. The fight's over. The clique wants to talk to you, if you'll go over and talk with us. You're voted in."

That seemed okay for me, but what about my buddy?

I pushed away from the wall and told Stubby to follow me. I walked toward the clique and had taken just a few steps when

Carl said, "You're invited, not the punk."

I told Carl that Stubby was my friend, and there was no way he was going to sit with the punks. I told him I appreciated being voted into the clique and, now that I was a member, it was my right to bring up to all the fact that my friend was not a punk, and no one could make him one.

"I'm the one who broke the rules," I said. "My partner didn't. Let him fight someone else. Then decide what happens."

I told Stubby to go back to the wall. I knew him well enough to detect the fear he tried so hard to hide. I doubt anyone else saw it. My buddy had plenty of guts, just no punch.

A choice was made, and the fight began. I had to sit there and watch my friend get whipped. I had no choice. Neither did he.

The fight lasted longer than I thought it would, since Stubby seemed unable to get the knack of it. But at one point, the other kid ran into a punch that Stubby had thrown and fell to the floor. For a moment, it appeared Stubby had gotten lucky, but his opponent stood back up.

It was then that I closed my eyes, not wanting to watch any longer.

Carl called out, halting the confrontation. While Stubby and the other boy stood watching each other, Carl walked over to the semi-straight clique. He spoke with someone there, and from across the room he asked Stubby if he'd like to sit there. Stubby looked at me.

I started to say something when Carl told me the two cliques interacted. I closed my mouth, knowing the problem was solved. I leaned back in my chair; the worst was over. I could relax for a moment.

Among members of the straight and semi-straight cliques, there were not nearly as many fights as between the punks and semi-punks. When it did happen, it usually began with whispered plans for a confrontation that sometimes took weapons to resolve. Those weapons were razor blades or bars of soap tied inside socks and swung at the head. Knives were rarely used because they were difficult, though not impossible, to obtain.

Within a couple of months, the casts were removed from my arms. It took awhile before I could use my hands normally, but I had no real need to use them on anybody.

A counselor assigned us to the maintenance ground crew, which consisted of straight clique members. Five days a week, we'd work with our boss, repairing things all over the institution. This job gave us access to everything inside the perimeter fence. I was able to get to know a lot of kids from other dorms and was kept informed of much of what was happening.

I met two guys who were using drugs and selling them to others. They asked me to go to an area where someone else had placed the drugs and smuggle the drugs back to them. In return, I would get 25 percent of the drugs.

There was a simple method of getting dope inside Preston. One of the kids' older brothers who lived in Ione would fill a handball with drugs and, two nights each week, sneak up close to the fence. Once the guard truck had passed by, the kid would toss the handball over the fence, aiming for some weeds by an old pump house. It was a very simple operation, and only three people — all kids — knew how the drugs were getting in.

Parents were always giving their children money on visiting days, so there was plenty of cash around. As a result, we all prospered from this arrangement.

I did not use drugs at that time. I sold them all. Escape was always on my mind, and Stubby and I were getting as much money together as we could, stashing it away in preparation for the day we'd find a way out.

The guard who drove a truck around the perimeter always carried a rifle with him. This fact was always denied to parents. The guard had a certain spot he used when he needed to take a leak. That spot was behind our dorm, and we saw the rifle clearly whenever he'd open the truck's door and step out to do his thing. It was unlawful for such weapons to be carried in or around CYA institutions. Only tear gas guns, axe handles and handcuffs were supposed to be used when there was trouble.

Anyone planning an escape took his life into his hands. In

addition, there was a rumor that administration encouraged families living near the institution to hunt down escaped wards. Preston offered $50 — big money then — for any kid they captured.

The trouble-free period ended one day when I couldn't find the drugs. Either the ball hadn't made it over or someone else had found the stash. My two partners didn't believe me. They told me I'd better find the drugs or they'd deal with me in the worst manner possible.

The next day, I looked again for the ball but couldn't find it. I was aware that both my partners were not the types to play games with. One was there for stabbing his father to death. The other had shot a cop and later stabbed a guard at Nelles.

I had no choice but to believe they intended to carry out their threat and would do so with a weapon. For several days I tried to think of a way to solve the problem, hoping they would find out I really hadn't taken the drugs. When our maintenance crew boss took us to the main kitchen, I had already made up my mind. I needed a weapon.

I kept my eyes open. The boss had been called to fix a meat grinder inside the butcher shop. While other members of the crew were intent on watching the grinder being repaired, I edged over to an open cabinet. It was filled with butcher knives and meat cleavers. I removed a large knife and put it in my waistband under my shirt.

No one saw what I had done. Later, I stashed it in the maintenance shop, where we met every morning to begin work. From that day on, I carried it with me wherever I went. I didn't need it when I was in my dorm; the two kids were in another one.

The day arrived when it all came to a head. The crew was digging up some bushes from around the school area. The bushes were to be replanted in front of the administration building. The kids assigned to school were allowed a smoking break every couple of hours. They were in the middle of one as we began removing the bushes.

Suddenly, I heard a sort of ringing sound.

I turned around to see one of my problems laying on the ground where Stubby had knocked him with a shovel. The other kid was rushing at me with a shovel intending to cause me some pain.

Counselors, guards and teachers were now yelling, trying to stop the confrontation. Once an altercation with weapons began, it didn't matter if staff members were present and hollering. They were not so brave as to try and take a weapon away from a kid. Not wanting to risk injury to themselves, counselors would usually remain at a safe distance while they shouted their orders.

Knowing this — and knowing that the seriously dangerous kids did not care if they were caught as long as they completed what they set out to do — made us realize we lived in an environment in which there was no protection from assault. If a kid is unable to stand up under such conditions and requests he be placed in protective custody, he is taken to solitary confinement. He remains there for the duration of his stay with the CYA. Once a child has confined himself to protective custody and then requests a return to his dorm, he is almost certainly beaten.

The kids who seek protective custody do so as a last resort. And those who choose to submit to the assaults and rapes do so as the only alternative to suffering the lonely hell they will experience in protective custody. What a choice.

As that boy rushed toward me with the shovel, I pulled the knife and jumped over a bush, positioning myself next to a tree. That made it impossible for the shovel to be swung without hitting the tree. The kid swung anyway and got lucky. The shovel's handle hit the tree, snapped in two, and the shovel head curved around the tree and sliced into my neck.

I stepped away from the tree and let the boy come at me with what was left of the shovel's handle. I ducked low, pushed toward him and slashed at his stomach. I missed. My body turned from the force of the swing, then I felt an arm go around my neck and another hand grab mine.

I looked down and saw a civilian shirt sleeve and knew a counselor, braver than most, had grabbed me from behind. I could also see another counselor holding the kid with the shovel. For now, the incident was over.

The counselor yelled at me to drop the knife. I let it go. He pulled me away and handcuffed me. I saw Stubby already cuffed. He was laying face down on the grass, looking at me from the corner of his eye.

Then it dawned on me. Stubby had saved my butt.

I stared at him, then experienced a deeply felt emotion I could not have explained at the moment. Later, I would understand it was an emotion I have rarely dealt with to this day — love for a very true and faithful friend.

Until that incident, Stubby had never been involved in an act of violence any more serious than a fistfight. He hadn't been made of the stuff it took to be vicious. He was the only kid I knew who didn't swear. That fact, I believe, taught me to refrain from using foul language as I grew up.

Stubby was also one of the few kids at Preston who had not gone through any of the state's other institutions. He had been committed to the Youth Authority for stealing a bicycle. His father had gone to court, refusing to take him home, and had told the judge that Stubby was incorrigible and needed to be taught a lesson. Stubby was learning a lesson all right, but I doubt it was what the judge or his father had in mind.

A van arrived, and we were taken to administration. From there I went to the hospital in town, where doctors stitched up my neck wound. When I returned to Preston, I experienced my first stay there in solitary confinement. It was something no kid forgets.

As I walked into the building, I saw it was built like the cell block in a prison, like you might see on television. There were two tiers on both sides of the entrance door, with 32 individual cells.

A counselor led me past the cells toward an office. On the other side of the office was another row of cells, exactly like the ones I'd just passed.

The floor looked like it had been made from large, square

rocks. They were red in color and had been waxed and polished to a bright shine. When I looked down, I saw my reflection.

Inside the office, the counselor told me to undress. He searched my body for contraband then gave me a nightgown that I slipped on over my head. It fit me like a dress. It was the only clothing I was allowed to wear — no underwear, socks or shoes — except when I was taken out on a chain gang six afternoons each week.

The counselor explained the rules to me. At no time throughout my confinement in solitary was I to talk. If I was caught, a day would be added to the 30 days I already had.

I was not allowed off my bed in the cell unless I needed to use the toilet or get my meal tray. A day would be added to my time if I was caught off the bed for any other reason.

At no time was I to stand at my cell door to look out the window. If I did so and was caught, two days would be added to my sentence.

If I refused to work on the chain gang, I would remain in solitary until I had worked a total of 24 days. If I disobeyed a staff order, three days would be added to my time.

There were counselors inside the solitary confinement building at all times. There were three shifts of eight hours each, during which a different counselor was on duty. A different counselor "observed" us during each shift. Every kid who did not violate a rule during that shift would have a "2" placed next to his name on the page of a log that contained his name, Youth Authority number and cell number. The log's pages were similar to those of a calendar. There were 30 squares, representing 30 days. That was the minimum number of days a kid would be there.

At the end of every 24-hour period, if the kid had not violated a rule, there would be three 2's in that period's square. That showed he had served one day without misbehaving. If there were only two 2's in the square, he had to serve one-third or eight hours of an extra day. If there was only one 2, he had to serve 16 additional hours.

Once a total of 90 2's had been earned — 30 days' worth — the kid was released from solitary. This system often meant it took a lot longer than 30 days for the kid to get out.

Picture those boys — lonely, scared, many still frightened of the dark — who should still have been at home with their families, sitting in solitary confinement for months at a time.

The counselor took me to my assigned cell and locked me inside. There was a toilet and a sink, bolted to the wall on one side of the cell. The bed was like nothing I'd ever slept on before. It was made of iron.

There was a window embedded in the back wall. It was impossible to see through the window, not only because it was covered with a heavy mesh wire screen that had been bolted over it, but it was also filthy from dirt that had caked up over many years. Below the window was an old steam radiator bolted to the wall. There was a knob, and I was able to turn it on and off.

A light was fixed into the ceiling, covered with the same mesh as the window. That light stayed on 24 hours a day.

As the counselor locked my door, he told me I'd get a mattress at 10 p.m. It would be removed from my cell at 6:30 every morning. I was beginning to realize I wouldn't be too happy there.

As soon as the counselor left, I went to my door's window and yelled for Stubby. He called back, and that gave me a good feeling he was near. He was in the cell across from me. We spoke a few words before the counselor nearly broke his neck running back to our cells. He shouted we'd just earned two added days plus a zero for his shift. When I told him he could take that zero and put it up his zero, he became really disturbed.

He returned a few minutes later with a firehose. He soaked me down real good, laughing all the while. Stubby was yelling at him and got soaked down, too. It was going to take us a long time to get out.

We were fed on paper plates. The spoon they provided was made of cardboard. The food was heaped into one pile. I never really knew what I was eating. I learned to eat by closing my eyes, holding my breath, and shoveling the food into my mouth. The spoon became soggy and useless halfway through the meal.

On my second day in solitary, after eating lunch, a counselor took me out of the cell and walked me to what appeared to have once been a mess hall. There, he gave me my regular clothes and told me to dress against the wall. Stubby was one of the last to be brought in. Once he was dressed, the counselor led us outside to an area a few hundred yards from the building. There were five large mounds of dirt. We were split into two groups. One group would shovel dirt into wheelbarrows and the other group would push the wheelbarrows to one large pile of dirt, dump the load and return for another.

Piles were moved and then returned, uselessly, relentlessly. We did this six days a week, from noon until 4 p.m. Every two hours, the counselor allowed us two minutes to drink from a nearby water hose.

It was not enough to dump the dirt at the base of the mounds. The wheelbarrows had to be pushed to the top and emptied. If a kid stopped to rest for a moment, he lost a "2" for that counselor's shift.

I thought I knew what hate was, but I didn't really know until I humped those piles of dirt in the hot sun. While I sweated and hurt, I became more and more bitter. That bitterness turned into a different kind of hate, a true hate.

I constantly battled to keep my hate under control. I kept thinking how nice it would be to beat a counselor or guard with a shovel, as they sat under a tree, relaxed in the shade, and watched us labor. We suffered as much from the heat as we did from the work. Once I came down with sunstroke.

If we were careful, though, we could whisper to one another as we worked. That was how Stubby and I resolved to make our escape.

The mounds of dirt were 10 yards from the inner fence. The counselors and guards, while they sat in the shade, were at least 25 yards from the dirt piles. There was a slim chance we could climb over the fences and get away.

One day, we took off running. We climbed the fence. At the top, the barbed wire cut into our hands and bodies, but we made it over the first fence.

"Stop!" a counselor yelled.

"Go! Go!" shouted the kids.

As it turned out, luck was on our side. Possibly there was a rule that a counselor had to remain guarding the other kids. No one chased us.

Stubby made it over the fence a few seconds before I did. I was snagged at the top and had to remove my shirt. I left it there as I dropped to the other side. That fence was 12 feet high, maybe higher, but we were both able to drop from the top without breaking any bones.

We sprinted across an open field toward some distant trees that could give us cover. I looked over my shoulder and saw both counselors yelling for us to return.

"They must be crazy," I thought.

If Stubby and I hadn't become lost in the woods that afternoon, we would have been captured before the day's end. It had been our plan to find a house to break into and stay for a while, or find a car with keys in the ignition.

During our first night in the woods, a situation occurred that caused me some heavy head trips. We had been running for hours and could go no farther. The night air was very cold, and I was without a shirt. That didn't make much difference, really. Stubby was fully dressed and was still shivering.

We had failed in our search for shelter, so we found an area that had leaves on the ground. There we laid down and covered ourselves as best we could with the leaves. Still cold, Stubby and I cuddled together to allow one another's body heat to warm the other. That helped, but it was impossible to sleep. As he and I laid there, face to face, hugging one another, I realized I had never been this close to my friend. We had never touched, except to shake hands, but I also realized I was becoming sexually aroused. To say the least, I was shocked.

I reached down to adjust myself, and the back of my hand brushed against Stubby. I discovered he was in the same condition. I glanced at his face as he opened his eyes to look in mine, and he blushed.

It was an awkward moment, and unexpected. My confusion became more pronounced when I felt Stubby unbutton my pants. He did this while he stared into my eyes, as if to ask if it was all right. While he touched me, I was thinking I loved him and wanted him to do it. I saw a question in his eyes, and I answered him when I unbuttoned his pants.

When we were finished, a bond had formed between us that hadn't existed before. Our act together had drawn us very close. What was remarkable was the fact we hadn't spoken during those moments. It had all been said and confirmed in another way.

When the sky began to lighten, we started walking. I asked Stubby if he'd ever done anything like that before. He blushed and told me he had not. We never spoke about it again.

We found a cabin that had been sealed tight for the season. There was food and clothing inside. It was there that we went further than masturbation. We explored one another in every way we could think of and seemed never to get enough of each other. I had never enjoyed anything as much before in my life.

The fears I have carried around with me have caused me much pain. Would anyone understand if I told them what happened between me and Stubby? I guess I'll find out soon, when members of my family read this and learn about it for the first time.

I have often wondered how it all worked out for Stubby and how it affected his life. I have thought about him and have prayed that our experience together — not just the sexual aspect — didn't cause him to live the mental hell that I experienced.

Nineteen days after we escaped, Stubby and I were caught shoplifting food from a small store, 30 miles from Preston. Three adults grabbed us as we left the store and called the police. If we had found clothing that actually fit us when we broke into the cabin, we would probably have been scolded and sent on our way. But we were still wearing our institution pants. That night, we were back at Preston, in solitary confinement.

We spent the first 30 days in our cells. We weren't allowed to work on the chain gang. We were unable to see or to talk to one another, because we had been assigned cells at opposite ends of the cell block.

After 30 days, we were allowed to work outside again. The counselors chained us together with leg irons. They placed one cuff around Stubby's ankle and one around mine. There was a 2-foot length of chain between us.

Out on the dirt, the counselors thought it was funny to have us both pushing the same wheelbarrow, instead of both just loading it. The work was rougher than usual for a while.

When we returned to our cells each afternoon, I found new spots where the steel cuff had rubbed away my skin. I had raw sores, many of which became scars that remain with me today. They serve to remind me, as numerous scars on my body do, of the hate that weighed me down more than any chain could.

Actually, without the hate, we could never have stood strong, with our heads high. Our hate served to take all they threw at us while we looked right at them, spit on the ground, and smiled. That pissed off the counselors more than any words could have.

Stubby and I kept our noses clean, did our work and were returned to F dorm after serving 60 days in solitary.

# ELEVEN

A lot of handshakes and back slaps greeted our return. Stubby was told he'd be sitting with the straight clique. It would have been that way even if I had to fight every one of them.

The counselors weren't too happy with us. Stubby and I couldn't walk from one room to the other without being ordered to stand for a search. During the searches, we were told to stop dead in our tracks. If we moved in any way, such as putting a hand in our pocket, we'd be sent to the hole.

Stubby and I quickly worked on another escape plan. We dared not complain about the harassment, to get them off our backs. By acting complacent and humble, we got the counselors to leave us alone. They congratulated themselves on finally breaking our spirits. The tactic worked so well that when the dorm captain was paroled a few months later, the kids were allowed to vote me into that position.

I made the counselors' jobs easier by keeping everyone in line and making sure their orders were obeyed. As dorm captain, I enjoyed privileges like no other boy in the house. I went to bed when I felt like it. I drank coffee from the counselors' coffee pot, and I walked around without the Man putting his nose in my business.

For all my privileges, I still hated making the counselors' jobs easier. Giving orders or being the tough guy whenever a problem arose wasn't my idea of fun. At any time of the day, a counselor might pull me aside and say, "Whip that kid's ass or have someone else do it."

I wanted the job for one reason: To make a nighttime escape from inside the dorm.

Stubby and I continued our affair. I appointed him dorm sergeant. This allowed us access to the sleeping area while the other kids were in the dayroom. We could do whatever we wanted without anyone catching us, or so we thought.

One evening, we were caught in the act by a counselor who always treated us right and seemed to actually like us. He often brought us cigarettes and other things we couldn't otherwise obtain. He was surprised to discover us laying together, but he left without saying a word. Ten minutes passed, and then he called me to his desk. I figured he had reported us and was now waiting for the van to take us to solitary.

Much to my surprise, he said he understood things like that happened when boys were locked up. He warned us that any other counselor would have sent us to the hole.

That counselor did us a favor in more ways than he might have known. Had he reported us, the hole would have been the least of our problems. Our status in the straight clique would have been seriously jeopardized, too, for obvious reasons.

I repaid the counselor the favor, though I doubt he ever realized it. Stubby and I had decided to escape on a Saturday night because the goon who drove the security truck around Preston didn't carry a rifle on weekends, or so we heard. We decided to jump on a Friday night, all because the friendly counselor didn't work Fridays. We didn't want to get him in trouble with his superior.

I had resumed my job on the maintenance crew, and arranged to have a kid's sister throw a package over the fence. The package was to contain four hacksaw blades. I gave the boy two twenties for his trouble.

I stashed the blades inside a shower drain by loosening the screws and removing the drain cover. Using a thin wire looped through the slit of the drain cover, I tied together the hacksaw blades and my knife, all enclosed in a plastic bag. All I had to worry about was a plumber being called in to fix a clogged drain.

One day, a notorious snitch came to roost in our dorm. He was big, though, and knew how to fight. His name was Snap, after a nervous habit he had of snapping his fingers. Two guys from the semi-straight clique jumped him, and he whipped them both without putting too much effort into it.

Snap presented a serious threat. The guy was obviously tough enough to take on anyone in the dorm, yet he could not be accepted as one of us because he was a snitch. At the same time, we were leery of jumping him.

Fear fluttered in my gut. As dorm captain, I was expected to deal with him. I knew I couldn't whip him in a fair fight or any other kind of fight. I wasn't sure I'd come out on top even if I creeped on him, and gave it to him on the back of his head.

This kid ran his mouth for a few long days. He talked about how tough he was and dared anyone to prove differently. Some of the guys must have been wondering if I was afraid of him. Well, I was. I was no King Kong. Still, I wasn't about to admit my fear.

A few guys were talking about taking him all the way out. Murder would put a lot of heat on the dorm and foul up my escape plans. It might also affect other things, like Stubby and me getting together and doing our thing.

I suggested to Snap that he request a transfer to another dorm. He was leery of my rep and told me that he didn't plan on transferring anywhere but felt we should be friends. I told him I'd heard he was a snitch and that a snitch could never be my friend. I was watching him closely and saw in his eyes the anger caused by that verbal slap.

Snap went on running his mouth, becoming bolder with every word. While the entire dorm listened, he told me the straight clique were a bunch of punks, and he was thinking about taking over. That was where he made his mistake.

The fear we all hid had been awakened by this fool. We dreaded confronting Snap, since losing a fight to a snitch would place the loser on the same level as the snitch. The fear of losing one's status was a greater fear than physical pain. The fear of losing face and status is the kind that creates the most violent confrontations.

It was up to the president of the straight clique to respond to Snap's statement. But I told Chris, the straight clique president, that as dorm captain, I should have already taken care of the problem. I told him the straight clique would have to let me deal with Snap or I would be forced to resign as dorm captain and give up my membership in the clique.

Chris agreed with me, very likely with a feeling of relief.

That same afternoon, I removed my shank from the drain and stashed it in my chair. I told all of the straight clique members how I intended to deal with Snap and what I wanted them to do.

Later, we sat out on the grass in front of the dorm, as we did each evening after mess hall. A counselor unlocked the dorm door, so those who needed to use the bathroom could do so, one at a time. The counselor sat on the grass and talked with any kid who had something to discuss with him. He paid litle attention to those who walked into the dorm.

Stubby and I went in and, while I removed the shank from the chair, Stubby took Snap's blanket off his bed.

Chris saw my signal and walked over to Snap to tell him that he should go to the dorm to fight. Fighting in the dorm during yard time was a popular thing to do, since there was little risk of going to solitary. As we'd expected, Snap accepted the challenge and headed inside.

Stubby held the blanket ready. Snap came through the entrance, and Stubby threw the blanket over him and yanked him from view of the others outside. I could hear Snap's muffled cries, but it was too late for him. I stabbed him several times in the stomach, down low, as I did not want to send him home in a box. The three of us fell to the floor.

Snap struggled for a moment, then laid still. I looked at Chris, now standing by the door. He indicated all was clear outside.

We left Snap laying there and stepped outside. No one, including our clique, was looking our way.

I wrapped the shank in a bandana and put it in a hole that some of the kids had dug for us. They filled the hole as Stubby and I laid on the grass and checked each other for blood. I cleaned some off my wrist with spit and dirt.

I was so wound up that all of my muscles felt like knots. Stubby whispered that he felt he was going to be sick. We waited for what might happen next.

We didn't have to wait long. Two minutes passed before a kid found Snap just as we had left him, the blanket over his head soaked with blood.

The boy screamed. The counselor ran to the door and fell on the shouting boy.

The counselor yelled for everyone to back away from the door and return to the grass. Within less than a minute, they had Snap on a stretcher in back of an emergency van and off to the hospital. They got Snap to the hospital fast enough to save his life.

All the kids were really talking it up. Many told tales about the violent acts they had "committed." But seeing Snap nearly bleed to death really gave them something to think about.

The kids soon became quiet. Members of my clique looked at Stubby and me with a sort of awe plastered on their faces. They looked away when I looked over at them. I stood there smelling their fear.

A dozen counselors were trying to keep us together on the grass. One yelled at me to get everyone into ranks of four and march them toward administration. I did what I was told, though I was feeling more than a bit sick. No glory, just shame. Had I not been a coward, I would have fought Snap and, if I lost, fought again, and again, until the problem was resolved to my satisfaction.

The incident caused me to withdraw even further into myself. I became less talkative, more difficult to draw into conversation. I had accomplished what all kids set out to do from the moment they are locked away — to place our peers and even members of our own cliques in total fear and awe.

Never again did I fear those around me, as I had before this incident. Fear would come only as a direct result of physical harm. And I used that fear to see me through the problem. From that day on, no one was allowed to know what I thought or what I felt (Stubby excepted). The quieter a kid, the more fear other kids have for him.

# TWELVE

One by one, we were led into a large waiting room and interviewed. The potential snitches had no idea who took out Snap. After five or six hours, the counselors led us back to the dorm and stayed with us the entire night.

Staff interviewed us all over again the next day. They found out Snap had been having trouble with the straight clique.

When a counselor grilled me about the problem, I told them the truth; that Snap's big mouth was upsetting the entire dorm. That I asked Snap to request a transfer to another dorm, and that he refused. That I intended to resolve our differences. Fighting was more or less an acceptable manner of handling problems and gave my statement the ring of truth.

The staff concluded I had nothing to do with the stabbing and probably had no idea who had done it. I was relieved that Stubby was not brought in during the second round of questioning.

A rumor began circulating that Snap would live. I was happy but concerned, because he knew Chris had set him up for the hit. He hadn't had enough time to see Stubby or me. If Snap snitched, staff would come down hard on Chris.

The counselors told us a "silent system" would be in effect until the investigation was concluded, but the straight clique talked quietly, anyway, and reached the conclusion that Chris was going to be fingered.

It was decided then that Chris would go in and tell the counselors he had been afraid to tell the truth but now felt it best to step forward and give them the "true story."

Chris was to say he had challenged Snap to a fight and they had gone inside the dorm. Chris heard a noise, turned around and saw a blanket being tossed over Snap's head. He wasn't able to see who was behind Snap and really didn't care. Fearing he was also going to be jumped, Chris ran back out to the grass, where he told his clique someone had tried to jump him. They all stood to go inside with him when another kid began hollering, and the counselor ran into the dorm. It was a lame story, but it was the best we could think of.

After Chris told this whopper, the staff's investigating team went into a room to discuss what they had heard. The entire clique was again questioned at length. We each told the same story. It was obvious the staff was frustrated.

Twenty minutes later, a dozen counselors handcuffed every member of the straight clique and took us to solitary and strip-searched us. We were told of a cell shortage, due to a problem in the black kids' dorm; dorms were segregated in those days. We were asked to raise our hands if there was any objection to two boys being assigned to each cell in solitary. No one raised their hand. We were allowed to choose our cell partner. My choice was Stubby.

We spent 33 days in the hole. I must admit we were treated better than usual. We were allowed to keep our mattresses at all times. And we were allowed to speak to our cell partners, as long as we did it quietly. We left our cells only for interrogation and showers.

During those weeks, Stubby and I came to know each other more intimately than we could have back in F Dorm. I'm not talking about sex, although that went on, too. I mean we got into each other's minds and shared things about ourselves that we had never shared with another person.

It would be a breach of trust to discuss the many things I learned about Stubby. I will say he was terribly abused during his short life. He felt I was the only person who gave a damn about him. I felt the same way about him. From Stubby and his experiences, I learned just how cruel this world can be.

The staff worked on us daily, trying to weaken our resolve to remain silent. The counselors would stop at the cell door and ask if we were ready to tell who had stabbed Snap.

We were able to learn more from them than they did from us. We learned Snap would definitely live, that he had said it was not

Chris who had stabbed him, and that he had no idea who had, except that he was sure it was someone from the straight clique.

On the 33rd day, a counselor told us to roll up our gear. We were being released from the hole. All of us were taken to administration and told we'd be assigned to different dorms. Nothing else mattered to me except getting out of solitary.

The counselors in solitary were glad to see us go. We didn't follow orders very well, and we often yelled out the cell doors, checking each other out. For lack of anything better to do, we'd kick the door. Other kids doing time would join us raising hell. We'd plug the toilets and flood the cells with water. It would flow out under the door, onto the tier and into other cells. It was difficult for the counselors to find out who actually perpetrated the flooding.

I guess we weren't punished because of their overcrowding problem. Even as we were escorted from solitary, we yelled out to those staying behind to keep telling the Man to kiss their rear ends. When the door locked behind us, we could hear the boys inside yelling at the counselors and kicking their doors.

While the superintendent decided where to assign us, Stubby and I began discussing our escape. A counselor soon informed us that we would all be returned to F dorm. The news went over well. Staff had obviously realized that assigning us throughout the institution would have caused other problems.

We walked out of the office and down a corridor. Then I saw the reason why we'd been let out of the hole. In one of the offices, surrounded by several counselors, sat Snap. The other guys didn't appear to notice him, and I didn't mention it. I looked into Snap's eyes and quickly looked away. I was feeling the guilt I'd developed by stabbing him. But guilt is a luxury a kid cannot afford while he's locked up.

When we entered F dorm things became very quiet. The semi-straight clique were sitting in our chairs. We took that as an insult. Those boys sure looked concerned. Without a word, they went back to their chairs as we sat in ours.

It was still silent as I walked over to the kid who was wearing the dorm captain's bars. I held out my left hand, palm up. I kept my right hand clenched in a tight fist. I expected some sort of protest to my silent demand. Without hesitation, the boy unpinned the bars from his shirt lapel and placed them in my hand. I noticed the counselor watching intently. I returned to my chair. Stubby pinned the bars on my shirt.

Everything returned to normal, except now there were two counselors working the day and swing shifts.

On Oct. 8, 1958, four days after my 16th birthday, Stubby and I cut through the steel frames that held the dorm's 5 by 8-inch windows. We cut through four bars and busted out four of those windows, removing the bars in one piece, now shaped like a cross. We cut a little each day and held the frame together with putty stolen from the maintenance shop.

Since all the guys in the clique had hung tough while in solitary and didn't snitch about the stabbing, I knew it was safe to tell them that I was checking out of our hotel again. They were welcome to come, if they wanted. Five of them jumped at the chance and agreed to run in a direction different from the one Stubby and I took.

We climbed through the window that night. We knew the counselor patrolling the grounds in the truck carried a rifle. I was scared. I heard of shots being fired once, when a boy tried to escape after returning from dinner.

Stubby was right behind me as I hid behind some bushes, about 40 feet from the first fence. The counselors had made their 2 a.m. count 10 minutes before we went out the window. We had an hour and a half before the next body count. The clique members who stayed behind promised to keep an eye on the other kids in case one tried to sound an alarm.

Long before our escape, we timed the counselor's rounds in his pickup at 17 minutes per lap. Like the other kids who escaped, Stubby and I had our blankets with us, to protect us from the barbed wire at the top of the fence.

Hiding in the bush, waiting for the truck to roll past, I began shaking like a cold, wet dog. Every muscle in my body was so tight that my limbs shook involuntarily. We watched the truck roll by, then we ran for the first fence. At the top, I threw my blanket over the fence. I went across the top without any problem but couldn't pull the blanket off the barbed wire.

We were supposed to hide the blankets to conceal our escape. Stubby yelled at me to forget it and get running. I left the blanket hanging there as I jumped and went over the second fence.

I ran through the open field like the devil was on my tail. I felt exhilirated to have beaten Preston again!

The field offered no place to hide ourselves. We had to reach a grove of trees set far away at the side of a hill before the guard in the truck made another round.

After running a long while, we reached the trees. I fell behind one, exhausted. I looked over at Stubby, who was on the ground a few feet from me, gasping for breath. He had a big grin on his face. We both felt good.

Moments later, I saw a flashing light, back by the fences. The counselor had spotted the blanket. Stubby and I had to get moving.

We jogged deep into the woods without stopping to catch our breath. We had prepared ourselves by running the track around the football field, and we were both in great physical condition.

By the time we stopped, were 10 miles into the forest. We were lost. But being lost was the least of our concerns. All we cared about was getting far enough away so we would have a chance at remaining free.

It would take many years before I realized the true meaning of the saying, "You can run, but you can't hide." Running wasn't the answer, but at the time our strongest urge was to run away from the people who abused us. Nothing changes. The children incarcerated today feel the same way.

Stubby and I spent five days and nights wandering through the woods. We had no food, but we were fully clothed and protected well from the cold night air. There was water, though, and I think that is the reason we survived. One day, Stubby killed a bullfrog and tried to eat its legs, raw. He gave up after gagging on the first swallow. I didn't try.

We hadn't thought to bring extra matches. We squandered the ones we brought on the first day, to light cigarettes. But we were smart enough not to light a fire. Smoke might have brought us unwanted attention.

On our fifth day, we spotted a pickup truck parked on a road. In the distance, I saw a man driving a tractor and figured the truck was his. The keys were inside, and, very quickly, so were we.

Speeding down the road, Stubby and I began to laugh; a laughter caused by our great sense of relief. We had walked over 100 miles. I had begun to wonder if we were going to come out alive. We hadn't eaten or slept much since our escape.

In a paper bag we found several sandwiches and an orange. There was a jar of orange juice on the floorboard. We had a feast, driving down that road, unable to recall anything that had tasted so good.

I drove for 15 or 20 miles before we began to see other cars and trucks. We reached the top of a hill and saw a small town below the grade. It was time to get rid of the truck. I parked it behind some trees off the side of the road. We walked toward town through a wooded area. I knew from experience that we shouldn't let anyone see us.

I thought of my parents and recalled that I hadn't seen them in two years. Stubby's dad would turn us in if we sought his help, but I felt my parents would not. We waited in the woods until dark, then walked into town and found a pay phone. Mom accepted my collect call but began to cry before I could say much. Dad took the phone and said the police already contacted him and told him of the escape, requesting he call them if he learned of my whereabouts.

I told Dad where I was anyway. He promised to drive the 200 miles to pick us up. I told him where to park so I could see him from our hiding place.

Five hours later, at about 2 a.m., I watched him drive up and park beside a cafe. He turned off the engine and sat in the car. I watched for several minutes to ensure no one was curious about Dad or his car. Those minutes felt like an hour.

Then, Stubby and I ran to the car and scrambled into the front seat. Before he said anything, Dad started the engine and drove out of town. Then he pulled the car to the side of the highway, stopped, and hugged me tightly and kissed me. It had been a very long time. I introduced Dad to Stubby. We were on our way home.

We arrived in Redding a few hours later. Dad stopped at a restaurant and ordered food to go. With our hair matted with dirt and twigs, and our clothes torn, we would have drawn attention had we gone inside the restaurant, so we stayed in the car.

Dad brought us steaks and potatoes, and they were a sight to behold. Meat is not commonly served inside institutions, unless within a stew. We ate the food and drank cold milk; I felt sure everything was going to be okay. It had been a long time since I felt so safe and secure.

Driving home, I saw Mom and Danny standing on the porch. Dad told me he thought it best if the other kids didn't know we had escaped. No one told them. If Danny reads this and remembers that night, he'll know for the first time how I got home.

Mom burst out crying as we hugged each other. She pulled away from me and looked at Stubby, who was a pathetic sight, then hugged him, too. She told us to go into the house.

Stubby and I went to the bathroom. I stared in the mirror at my badly scratched face. My hair looked like anything but hair. We jumped into the shower and scrubbed each other's back. Dad brought us clean clothes.

We dressed in our fresh clothes and walked into the living room. Danny stared at me. It had been several years since he'd seen me, and we didn't know how to approach each other. At last, we said hello.

Mom sat on the couch next to me and tried to brush the knots out of my hair. It was an impossible task. She had to cut our hair quite short.

Danny introduced us to his girlfriend Rita. I cannot recall if she and Danny were married yet. But she knew all about his brother, the black sheep of the family. Rita was a beautiful girl.

She sat close to Danny while we all talked. I could sense she was frightened of me. Whenever I looked directly at her, she looked away.

Mom and Dad took Stubby and me outside. They told us we couldn't stay with them, since the police would find us if we did.

It was decided that they would drive us to Red Bluff in the morning and put us on a Greyhound bus. We would go to Texas, where friends of the family lived. Dad already telephoned them and explained the situation. The family friends had agreed to let us live there until we were 18 and no longer under the jurisdiction of the CYA.

Danny and Rita were living in a trailer next to my parents' house. The trailer had an enclosed porch. Stubby and I fell asleep there, laying on sleeping bags my parents had put down for us. Several hours later, which really felt like minutes, Dad shook me awake. He said a police car had just turned into the driveway. We had to get out of there.

Stubby and I got away quickly. This time, I knew the area and was not worried about being caught in the miles of thick brush that surrounded the house. We ran for a half mile or so, then stopped and rested. We sat on the ground, listening for any sound that would indicate we were being chased.

Later that morning, I went back to the house alone and asked my parents if they could give us some money. Dad still wanted to take us to Red Bluff, but I knew how sneaky cops could be. If they were going to catch me, I didn't want my family with me.

Dad gave me $200, all the money he had on him. Mom was crying. She gave me lots of hugs and wet kisses. I thought I detected a bit of wetness in Dad's eyes, too, but I wasn't sure.

They walked me to the edge of the clearing. I didn't look back as I ran into the brush and headed back to Stubby.

I was feeling lost and very much alone. I wanted to stay with my family so badly. I moved deeper into the brush, thinking of Mom and Dad.

A week later, the police spotted us driving south in a stolen car. We had intended to cross the border into Mexico. Near San

Diego, with just six or seven more miles to the border, I heard a siren. I tried to outrun the cop but slammed into a truck that was loaded with hay.

Although we were speeding more than 70 miles an hour when we smacked the truck, Stubby and I received only cuts and bruises. We spent the night in the hospital and the next four inside Los Angeles County Juvenile Hall.

Three of Preston's counselors drove south from Ione to pick us up. It was no great surprise when we were escorted directly back to solitary.

# THIRTEEN

No one spoke to me — counselor or guard — for three days. On the fourth day, two guards clamped me in leg irons and belly chains and escorted me to administration.

The staff recommended our transfer to Deuels Vocational Institute, in Tracy. They said Stubby and I were "incorrigible."

Webster's dictionary defines incorrigible as, "That which cannot be corrected or reformed, especially because it is set in bad habits." No child who is loved, understood, and given proper guidance will become "incorrigible" at such an age. It's easier to throw away a child who reacts to his abuse than attempt to heal his pain. Are children born "incorrigible"?

I was not allowed out of my cell for anything but a shower for close to a month. Once a week, Mom and Dad were allowed to visit me. I complained of my treatment in solitary, and my parents in turn complained to administration. Dad threatened to sue if the counselors continued to lock me up 24 hours a day.

The staff relented, giving me the job of cleaning the building's floors. While the other kids worked the chain gang, I swept, mopped and buffed the floors until they shined like mirrors.

The buffer weighed at least 20 pounds, but I welcomed the hard work, slinging the machine back and forth across the floor. The work built the muscles in my arms and shoulders and was a good substitute for lifting weights. I was allowed a five minute break each hour, but I would work right through them. I felt stronger, both physically and mentally.

I frustrated the counselors, who liked to hone in on a kid's weakness. Maybe I intimidated them. Whenever they weren't protected by a cell door, they no longer copped an attitude.

When I was out of my cell, the counselor on duty was supposed to keep me in sight at all times. He'd usually get bored and return to his office to sit and smoke. This enabled me to go and speak with Stubby. I'd sneak him cigarettes I was able to rip off from a counselor's coat pocket.

I was worried about going to Deuels, where, I had heard, kids were celled with adults. Stubby and I admitted to each other that we were scared. We weren't the vicious incorrigibles that administration had claimed us to be. We had been forced to protect ourselves from becoming punks.

Staff wanted us caged. They took personal offense to our escape attempts. We were expected to accept the murder of our souls. The kids whose spirits are broken and simply accept their fate like lambs at the slaughterhouse can no longer function properly in the world outside. Does this sound like a catch-22?

During our stay in solitary, we met a kid who was being held in protective custody. Kids in one of the dorms had beat him into pulp and then raped him repeatedly. The boy was deaf and dumb. I felt sorry for him.

Kids in protective custody were allowed a pencil and paper. The boy wrote me a note, asking if I would give him a cigarette. As a member of a straight clique, I wasn't supposed to have anything to do with a kid in protective custody. We were never to consort with a snitch or a punk.

Yet I gave him a smoke. Over time, I even began to understand him a little, through sign language. He told me he had been in protective custody for three months and was very lonely. Three months was a long time for a 15-year-old boy to be in an empty cell. He wasn't allowed to leave his cell for any reason other than a shower or to visit with family. His only relative was an abusive father who did not visit him.

I suggested that he ask staff to assign him to K dorm, where many of the younger, physically weak boys were housed. At first, he expressed fear at being returned to the main population. But one day he passed me a note saying he was going to K dorm. I wished him luck. When I came out of my cell the next day to clean the floors, his cell was empty.

Four days later, he was returned to protective custody. He had been badly beaten and gang raped by a bunch of black kids. He had been assigned to work in the main kitchen. His first day there, two guys forced him to orally copulate them in the bathroom. They approached him the next day for sex. Through gestures, he told them he didn't want to do it anymore. Shortly afterward, eight guys beat and raped him.

The deaf and dumb boy had been sent to Preston for having stolen his father's car after his father beat him in a drunken rage. And his father pressed charges.

The boy told the authorities about the abuse, but his father denied it. The authorities believed the father and sent the boy to Preston. He was to be confined there until it was decided he was rehabilitated.

During his four and a half weeks at Preston, the boy had been assaulted and raped at least 20 times. I am sure he was grateful to his father and the juvenile court for his chance at rehabilitation.

He began to act strangely, and it became difficult for me to help. One day, walking past his cell door, I saw him cutting deep gashes into his face with a bed spring. He was a bloody mess. Though I tried getting his attention, he ignored me. I stood there and watched. I couldn't go to the Man.

When I came out of my cell the next day, the boy was gone. He was back in protective custody a week later. He didn't look pretty anymore. No doubt that was his intent.

He no longer communicated with me. Usually, he sat on the floor, staring at the back wall.

On the 10th day after his return, he slipped me a note. It said he was thinking about killing himself. I was reading it when a counselor grabbed the note and read it. Knowing the boy couldn't hear him, the counselor announced that the boy had better calm down or he'd be put in the rubber room. The rubber room had nothing in it other than a hole in the floor that served as a toilet.

The counselor ordered me to not talk with anyone. I went to the second tier and began buffing the floor.

My gut started telling me something was wrong. I looked around, expecting to see the Man creeping up on me. There was no one in sight. A few minutes later, I worked my way over to where I could look from the top tier down into the deaf boy's cell, as I had done many times before.

I dropped the buffer and ran downstairs to his cell. His face was purple. He had taken a sheet, torn it into strips, woven them together, tied one end to the radiator and the other to his neck. Then he must have leaned his weight onto the sheet, strangling himself.

Not knowing what to do, I ran to Stubby's cell and told him what had happened. Stubby told me to get the Man.

The counselor ran to the cell and yelled at me to dial a number on the telephone and tell whoever answered what had happened. I did that, hung up the phone and looked down into the partially opened desk drawer.

Inside was a knife, the kind used to cut tar paper. It had a short, curved blade. I put it in my armpit, clamping it tightly in place to keep it from falling to the floor.

I returned to the cell. The counselor, to his credit, was trying to revive the boy.

It took the emergency crew 15 minutes to arrive. By then, the counselor had given up on the boy but had remained kneeling at his side. The counselor had a shocked expression on his face.

When the hospital staff arrived, I was locked into my cell. Later, I was taken to administration and interrogated about the incident. I told them about everything, except the suicide note and the counselor's callous reaction. We weren't supposed to snitch on staff members, either.

The next day, the counselor took me into his office and gave me a cup of coffee and a smoke. This was completely against the rules.

He asked me what I had told the investigators. He was very worried. Had I told his superiors about the note, he probably would have lost his job.

I told him I hadn't snitched on him. I became very bold as I watched the relief spread over his face. I told him I would keep quiet about the facts as long as he returned the favor in a manner acceptable to me.

He wasn't crazy about being blackmailed, but it was obvious to us both that he didn't have much choice. I asked for a pack of cigarettes each day he came to work. And I told him he'd have to cut me some slack about talking to people while I was working. Considering the situation, it was not asking too much, and he knew it.

He nodded his head, and that was the end of our conversation. He never again bothered me or gave me an order, except to tell me to return to my cell. I continued to do my job well, and no one had any complaints.

Stubby thought it was all very funny. When I told him about the knife I stashed, we began talking again about escape. We knew we didn't have much time to do what no one had ever done — escape from Preston's solitary confinement.

I had a difficult time getting over the suicide, but in the meantime, Stubby and I plotted our escape.

On D-day, the same counselor who let the deaf boy die was working. He and I had a score to settle. After I was let out of my cell for work, I hurried to the spot where I had stashed the knife and removed it.

I gave Stubby a signal. He tore his sheet into strips and tied them to the radiator, as if he was committing suicide like the other boy had done. I ran to tell the counselor that Stubby had killed himself.

The counselor ran to Stubby's cell. I was right behind him as he entered it. He knelt down and Stubby rolled over and punched the man in the face. I pulled his head back and put the knife to his neck. The counselor felt the cold blade. He didn't move.

Stubby used the sheets around his neck to tie up the man, who was telling us over and over that we were making a big mistake. I told him I'd kill him if he didn't shut up. He did.

I stuffed a sock into his mouth, then tied a strip of sheet over it. I'd seen it done in the movies. It worked almost too well.

Taking his keys, we locked him inside the cell and headed for a locker room where our regular clothes were kept. We removed our longjohns and slipped into our institutional issue. Then I remembered we'd forgotten the counselor's wallet. I went back to the tier, and some of the other kids began yelling at me to let

them out. It was a good thing I'd returned to the cell.. The counselor's face was purple. So much for the movies.

I admit considering for a moment to let him suffocate. But by
the time I had his wallet, I decided to remove the gag. I thought
about the boy he allowed to die and kicked myself for not having
the guts to kill him.

I took off from the cell, and the idiot started yelling. He was
not too bright. I went back inside, held the knife to his throat and
cut him, just a little. I told him if he opened his mouth again, I'd
make sure he would not say another word for the rest of his life
— all three minutes of it.

I unlocked several cell doors and handed the keys to some
kid, instructing him to let out anyone else who wanted to go. I
finished dressing and retrieved the keys from the kid. Stubby and
I flew out the back door. We climbed the fence, which was just a
few yards from the building. Since no wards were ever allowed on
the grounds around solitary, the surrounding fence had no barbed
wire across the top.

We sneaked across an open area behind the administration
building, then squatted behind a large tree. As I looked around to
see if there was anyone on the side of the hill near the parking
lot, I had to piss so bad I could taste it. But I was too tense to go.

Stubby asked me why I was smiling. I was thinking we had
really beat the Man this time, and in a way that would be talked
about for a long time, no matter the outcome.

We took off down the hill, running full speed. There was
nothing to hide us from the sight of someone exiting the castle.
We had to cover a quarter mile before we reached the beginning
of the woods, where we had become lost twice before.

Someone yelled. I turned and saw a woman stop her car in
the middle of the road. I told Stubby to stop, and he looked at me
like I'd lost my mind. I told him to act like we were giving ourselves up.

I was certain the woman was unaware what we were doing
out there, since some of the kids were trusted to work outside
the compound during the day. She seemed confident. Even if we

were doing something wrong, she felt she had nothing to worry about. Escape attempts were never violent. Two kids using a knife to subdue a counselor was unheard of.

"Stop where you are!" the woman shouted. "Come here! What are you doing?"

She spoke in the tone of a scolding mother. She looked completely surprised when instead of replying, I simply pulled my knife and said, "Lady, you better do what I say."

I forced her into the passenger's side of the car. I climbed into the back seat, positioning myself behind her. Stubby quickly turned the car around and headed off.

After 30 miles of listening to this woman snivel, I told her I'd watched her spank kids with a paddle until their bottoms bled. Teachers at Preston found the paddle indispensible.

I put the knife to her throat.

"You want to know what it feels like to bleed?"

She shook her head.

"Then you best shut up."

The woman's sadism came to mind. Whenever she caught some boy doing something she objected to, she would call for a male counselor.

While he bent the boy over his knee, she would paddle the child in front of the class. Before she was done, spots of blood would soak through his pants.

After driving about 50 miles, far from any place we recognized, I told Stubby to pull the car to the side of the road. I wanted to get rid of the old bag. Besides, Stubby's driving made me nervous.

He stopped, and I told the woman to get out. She picked up her purse and opened the door. When I told her to leave the purse, she tried to unzip it.

I grabbed the purse away from her. She wouldn't let go, and I had to grab her hair to force her it from her. Stubby took the purse as I pushed the woman from the car.

Inside the purse I found a small .25-caliber pistol. I knew counselors who carried large pocket knives, like the one at Nelles who stabbed the boy in the chest. Staff consistently carry weapons now. One is a heavy, steel flashlight, used primarily as a billy club. They are legal, as are clubs, Mace, handcuffs and chains.

Stubby and I both knew we weren't interested in keeping the gun. A few miles down the road, I tossed the pistol and purse out the window, after I removed what little money was in it.

We drove clear to Redding, then hid the car in dense brush just off the road. We got to my parent's house quickly. I called out to Mom, who was working in the yard. She ran to meet us and started to cry. I didn't have to tell her we had escaped. The cops always did that for me.

There is no way to describe the feeling of entering your own home after doing time in a reformatory like Preston, to be hugged by those who care for you, instead of being abused by those who want to harm you.

I found Dad sitting on the couch. He held out his arms to me. I felt the comfort and safety I had known as a little boy, so many years ago. His body began to shake, and I pulled away to look at him. There was wetness in his eyes. His first words to me were, "Are you hungry?"

Dad gave Stubby a big hug. Then I got a shock. Stubby burst out bawling. He held Dad tightly. It had been a long time since a father figure had hugged Stubby. I stood there feeling a lump in my throat, not really knowing if I could cry anymore.

It was just the four of us, sitting at the dining room table, enjoying a lovely dinner Mom cooked for us.

Suddenly, a voice shouted, "Freeze! Don't move!"

It was just like the movies.

I was caught with a fork in my mouth. That's where it stayed as I looked to my side and saw several cops, their guns drawn, aimed at Stubby and me. Someone put a choke hold on me and dragged me from the chair. I saw the same thing happen to Stubby before I was thrown to the floor and held there, a knee dug into my back.

Mom was screaming at the cops not to hurt us. She cried as

they pulled my hands behind my back and handcuffed me. They pulled me to my feet, holding each arm firmly.

I looked over at Mom. She stood with her back against the wall, holding her hand over her mouth. Dad was still sitting there in his chair, a cop's hand on his shoulder. In his eyes I saw so much pain.

"Where's the gun?" one cop asked me.

"Long gone," I said.

They let Mom and Dad hug and kiss us, then they took us to Shasta County Jail. On the way there, one cop said the woman's car had been spotted from the side of the road. It wasn't difficult to figure out where we'd gone.

The next time we escaped, we wouldn't head for home. Already, I began to plan for that day.

Stubby and I were put in the same cell, where we stayed until the next afternoon. Two Preston counselors handcuffed us and walked us to a waiting car. As I leaned over to get into the back seat, I felt a sharp blow to the back of my neck and fell face first on to the seat.

I struggled to sit upright and heard a scuffle outside. One of the cops told the counselors, "Children aren't beaten in my town." Stubby got in, the door slammed shut, and we were on our way back.

At Preston, staff chatted over old times with us. After our conversation, both my eyes were swollen shut and my right ring finger was busted. It is still crooked today. Stubby was beaten badly but suffered no broken bones.

Four counselors dragged us to solitary. I was stripped naked and thrown into the rubber room. Years later, I learned it became known as the quiet room. Nothing inside it has changed.

Like any kid held there, I was totally naked and was given a blanket at night to sleep on. It was pitch black inside, and cold.

I was let out twice in six weeks; once for a shower and once — the same day — for an interview with two detectives from the Ione Police Department.

They wanted me to tell them about the kidnapping of the

school teacher and the stealing of her car. I declined to discuss the incident. They tried to convince me that Stubby had told them all about it and had agreed to testify against me. They said Stubby had told them the whole thing was my idea. They said it would make things easier on me if I cooperated with them.

I stared at them and remained silent. They tried the bad-cop, good-cop routine. When that failed, they both punched me once, then returned me to solitary.

A week later, a counselor told me to come out of my cell. It was the first time that week the door had been opened for any reason. There was a slot in the door used for feeding; it was opened only to put a plate of food inside the cell.

The lights on the tier hurt my eyes as I stepped out. The counselor handed me a pair of longjohns and took me to his office where several counselors were sitting. They asked me if I had learned my lesson.

When I didn't respond, they told me no charges would be filed against me or Stubby. They said the director of the CYA had decided to give us another chance and not have us sent to Deuels.

I sat staring at them and their false smiles. One asked me how I felt about the decision.

Had I told them what I felt, that I wanted to kill them, they would not have let me out of that cell.

I wanted to tell them how I had kept myself from losing my mind; how I pulled a loose tooth, tossed it up in the air, then searched for it on my hands and knees, for hours at a time. Once, when I couldn't find it, I figured it must have fallen down the toilet hole.

I wanted to tell them how I smelled my own filth and how many times I went thirsty because the counselors "forgot" to give me water.

Sitting there, I told them what they wanted to hear; that I had learned my lesson, would be a good boy and would do whatever they wanted me to do. I said I wouldn't try to run away again nor would I cause more trouble if allowed to return to my dorm.

They smiled and nodded, pleased that they had brought a

serious problem child to his knees. They told me they were happy to learn I had seen the error of my ways. They said I would be returned to F dorm that afternoon.

Although it was uppermost in my thoughts, I did not ask them what they would do with Stubby. To my surprise, we were both taken back that day to F dorm.

Sitting in the back of the van that drove us there, Stubby reached over and squeezed my hand. He knew I had been through hell. I must have looked it, too. I leaned over and whispered in his ear. He laughed. I'd told him we'd be out in a month.

Stubby wished me happy birthday. I'd forgotten it was October, that I had turned 17 while I sat in the stripped cell. His greeting made me think of all the birthdays I'd missed since the nightmare had begun, eight long years ago.

# FOURTEEN

The dorm was silent as we entered. Then, members of the straight clique began clapping. Suddenly, everyone in the dayroom was doing the same. Some of the kids walked over to us, shook our hands and slapped us on the back.

I was still in a daze after spending so much time in the rubber room. It put a strange spin on everything, as if I was seeing things from a distance.

The counselor yelled for quiet. He ordered Stubby and me to his desk and told a guard to keep watch on the kids in the dayroom. The counselor took us to the sleeping area and let us know that the slightest trouble would put us back in solitary. I stared at him, saying nothing. Something in my look made him uncomfortable. He couldn't look me in the eye.

He had no intention of hassling us, he said, he just didn't want any trouble while he was working. I understood his problem. The guy was scared of us. Here were two kids who grab a counselor at knifepoint, rip off his keys, go over the fences, kidnap a staff member, leave her in the middle of nowhere, then go about their business. I could smell his fear. Frankly, I couldn't understand why they let us out of solitary.

Stubby and I were assigned beds next to each other. I more or less insisted on that. We returned to the dayroom and walked over to our clique. A couple of new boys were sitting in our seats. The president told them to move.

The new president's name was Newcomber. I had a gut feeling that he didn't belong with the straight clique, but didn't voice my opinion because I had no way to back it up.

Years later, I was to learn that I could survive only if I went with my animal instincts. Sometimes I would be wrong, but I preferred to be wrong than ignore something and get hurt, or killed. Most of the time, my gut proved itself correct.

Newcomber soon proved me right.

All of us talked for awhile. In the eyes of our peers, Stubby and I were heroes. We had guts. Silently, I understood it was more a matter of desperation than guts. I didn't say this out loud. I had to keep up my image.

After dinner, Stubby and I walked off by ourselves to discuss our next move. We had no intention of staying put.

We concluded that we'd need help from the guys in the clique if our new escape plan was to succeed. Three of them had checked out with us during the last escape. But Newcomber bothered me, and I told Stubby so. I couldn't give him a reason for my feeling. Stubby thought I was wrong.

I came up with a plan to see if my gut was lying. I told Newcomber that I had a gun smuggled in. I said the other guys thought I should tell him, in case he wanted to escape with us. I dropped him the phony information on where I was hiding the gun. Then I sat back and waited. I'd give it a couple days to see if anything happened.

Newcomber did not disappoint me. It took but a few hours. A group of counselors, headed by the assistant superintendent, raided the dorm. They tore apart the alleged hiding place. They questioned everyone, except me and Stubby, about the gun.

As the entire clique hung out that evening, I told the guys how I had smoked out a rat in the straight clique. I watched Newcomber fidget. The others were craning their necks, trying to see who I was talking about. Newcomber probably thought that as president he was protected. After all, who would suspect or doubt our great clique leader, the one who could be trusted at all cost?

I watched him squirm like a worm. There was nothing, then or now, I detested more than a guy who would rat on his friends and peers — one who sought to gain favor with the same people who kept him locked away.

Everyone was watching me closely. I hadn't yet named the rat.

I stood and turned, my back to Newcomber, and hovered over another kid. A look of confusion spread on his face. I winked at him then spun around. I kicked out with my right foot, catching Newcomber flush on his jaw. The bone snapped like a twig, and the sound was heard throughout the dayroom. There was no such thing as a fair fight. Especially when eliminating a rat.

It was all over with that one kick. Newcomber never got a chance to defend himself. In adult institutions, rats are killed instead of beaten.

Newcomber was taken to the hospital, and then it was business as usual. The counselor who warned me not to be a problem ignored the incident.

There was not much debate over who would be the new president and dorm captain. I walked over to the dorm captain and told him, "Those bars belong to me."

I expected a fight, and he made a mistake when he handed me the bars without one. He should have fought. There was no shame in losing a fight, as long as you proved how big your heart was. When he gave me the bars, he gave up the right to sit with us. He was demoted to the semi-straight clique.

In the next few months, Stubby and I made our plans for what would be our final escape. Back on the maintenance crew, we spent our few unsupervised moments working on a hole that we had begun to dig outside the equipment shack, under its floorboards. We spread most of the dirt out in the weeds around the structure. The other kids on the crew — all members of the straight and semi-straight cliques — helped us.

Once the hole was large enough to fit ourselves inside, we smuggled several jars of water and some bags of candy to the shack and hid them in the hole.

One day, when the crew boss was off somewhere, the time came for us to do our thing. Stubby and I slipped into the hole. The other boys covered the hiding place with a sheet of plywood. They spread dirt on top of the board, hiding anything that looked suspicious.

We laid there in the hole, side by side, and listened to the crew boss take roll call. When he called my name, there was no response. He called it again.

"Where the hell is Abbott?" he asked. "And where the hell is Stubblefield?"

I heard him say, "Oh, shit," and I suppose he then realized we checked out of our hotel again. I heard him as he yelled into a nearby telephone, "That little shit did it again. What the hell do you think I mean? He took off!"

Stubby started to giggle, and I had to hold my hand over his mouth. He almost caused me to laugh, too.

Several times during the next two days and nights, while we lay hiding in the ground, we heard staff members enter the shack to search for us. We must have seemed to have disappeared in a puff of smoke.

We figured they'd spend a lot of time searching the institution, unable to determine how we left it. Their gut feeling continued to lead them to the shack. We even heard the grill being pried off so they could look in the area beneath the floorboards.

We decided to make our move the night they lifted lockdown status, when the other kids returned to work crew. On our third day of hiding, we heard the other boys outside. Lying in that hole had not been easy. After the first day, we had to lift a corner of the plywood for fresh air, and were unable to cover that corner with dirt.

In our planning, Stubby and I forgot we'd need to answer the call of nature. We dumped one of the water bottles and peed into it, rather than pissing on each another. Once that bottle was full, we drank the other until it was empty, then slowly filled it again. By the time we heard the kids outside, we had run out of places to go.

Someone stomped hard on the floor, signaling the search had ended.

That night, we came out of our hole, then broke a window so we could get into the shack. We needed to use its toilet awfully bad; we needed a rake, too.

Administration had since concluded that barbed wire was not enough to discourage escapes. So, they had the top few feet of the inside fence covered with a heavy gauge mesh wire. It was impossible to climb. The rake we took from the shed would eliminate that little obstacle.

Reaching the first fence, Stubby and I jammed the rake into the wire mesh as close to the top of the fence as possible. Pulling ourselves up the rake's handle, hand over hand, we reached the top and were gone again. I hurt my foot after landing on the free side of the second fence. I learned later that I fractured two toes and my heel bone.

At first, it wasn't difficult to walk, but within an hour or so, the pain had become unbearable. I didn't tell Stubby. He noticed it, though, when we were about 10 miles into the woods. He got mad because I stayed quiet about it. I knew he would have wanted to stop and baby me or find a car to steal, even though we had decided to walk over the hills and not rip off anything that someone could later find. We knew that would lead the cops right to us. We were learning from our mistakes.

But we stopped and made a big mistake, anyway. He helped take my shoe off. My foot was a mess. It was black from bruising and had swollen to nearly twice its normal size. We couldn't get the shoe back on my foot. I stood and found it almost impossible to put any weight on it. Using a branch as a cane, I slowly followed Stubby deeper into the forest.

As if my foot was not enough to worry about, snow fell on our second night out. The way things were going, there was no way we were going to get out of there alive.

Stubby's face and hands were turning blue. We walked on. We wanted nothing more than to lay down and go to sleep, but we knew that would be fatal. When I began to think how comfortable a cell in solitary would be, I knew we were in real trouble.

After walking for more than a dozen hours through the snow, I heard the distant whine of a chainsaw. It was a beautiful sound. It was difficult to determine the direction from which it came, until we reached the top of a hill and found a farm below us.

Slowly, we made our way down the hill, walked behind a barn and entered through a back door. Inside, we sat down on bales of hay. The body heat of horses and cows inside some stalls had warmed the barn. It felt like a room with a blazing fireplace.

I laid back, totally exhausted. I dozed off, and I dimly remember Stubby covering me with a foul-smelling blanket. The next thing I knew, I was being shaken awake. I opened my eyes and saw a man, in his early 50s. I woke Stubby, who was laying beside me under the blanket. He looked at me, then at the man. The expression on his face asked me, "What now?"

"What are you doing here?" the man asked.

"We got lost after it started to snow," I said. "We came here to get out of the cold."

He asked me why we hadn't gone to the house instead; I didn't have an answer. In fact, I didn't respond at all. That must have made him suspect there was more to the situation than I was telling him.

He took us into the house and, noticing my limp, asked to look at my foot. I told him I'd hurt it when I slipped and tumbled down the side of a steep hill. A woman came into the room and offered us food.

While we waited to eat, the man kept looking closely at my foot. "You'll have to see a doctor," he said.

His questions continued. Our answers were not the best. He knew we were lying, and I figured he was beginning to suspect that we were from Preston. It turned out he thought we ran away from home. I didn't know then that we walked over a hundred miles. Without food, very little water and a badly injured foot, we'd come a long way in a short time.

I limped to the kitchen to eat. Stubby and I discussed our alternatives while the man sat in the front room. We decided to steal the man's truck the first chance we got. We weren't stupid enough to think he believed our story.

After the meal, we sat wrapped in blankets while our clothes dried in front of the fireplace. The man asked if we had run away from home.

"Yes, sir," I said.

"Well, I'm the pastor at the local church, and I want to help you any way I can. I think it would be best if I called your parents."

It suddenly dawned on me that Dad would play along with our story. I fell back on my chair as I limped to the telephone. The pain in my foot was so intense I couldn't stand up. My foot warmed, and the feeling returned. I wished it hadn't.

The man brought me the phone. I called home and Mom answered. I asked her if Dad was there; she said he wasn't. She asked me where I was, and I asked the man if he'd tell her. Before I handed him the phone, Mom asked if the man knew we'd escaped. I said no then handed the phone to him.

I winked at Stubby. Things were going to be okay. The man and Mom talked for awhile. He told her we could spend the night there. He said he'd drive us into town in the morning and put us on a bus for Redding.

During the rest of the evening, the woman soaked my foot in warm water and wrapped it with strips from a bed sheet. While she did this, the pastor read passages from the Bible and told us about God.

Many people before him shoved God down my throat until I gagged. I asked myself what kind of merciful, loving God would allow me, and so many like me, to be locked away, beaten, raped and treated like anything but a child of the human race. As far as I was concerned, there was no God, and no one would ever convince me with words that there was.

All the chaplains sounded like tape recordings. I asked them very direct questions a couple of times, seeking a reason for what I was going through.

"It's God's will," they would say. "Someday, it will be revealed to you."

Well, I figured, if it was God's will that I be beaten, raped, abused and treated like an animal, then God should be down on His knees, asking for forgiveness, instead of the other way around.

Today, my belief in God is very strong. But the Christian people have disappointed me. I wish they would read their bibles and learn what Jesus said about God's little children. Shame on all of us for letting His little children suffer as they do, so painfully and needlessly.

The next morning, the preacher's wife served us breakfast, and then the preacher drove us into town, stuffing us full of his God once again.

"I prayed to Him and asked Him to help you boys," he said, looking down the road. "I asked Him to forgive your sins, so when you leave this world you won't go to Hell and burn for eternity."

I wanted to tell the smug hypocrite that I was only 17 and had been living in Hell for eight years. I wanted to tell him the only merciful thing that could happen to me was if I was to die.

Instead of going to the bus station, he tricked us by driving straight to the cops. Stubby threw open the door and dove for the ground. When I hit the ground, I could barely hobble, let alone run. Without help, I couldn't even stand.

Several cops had been waiting by a glass door. As I tried to get up with Stubby's help, they opened the door and ran outside. I yelled to Stubby to run.

He wouldn't let go of my arm. Stubby was a fast runner and would have made it if he had run instead of worrying about me.

While we sat inside the jail's holding cell, waiting for the Preston counselors to come get us, Stubby told me he had nowhere to run without me. I learned a lesson from Stubby that day. I have never turned my back on a friend in trouble.

After the actions of the preacher that day, it took a very special couple to guide me to the Lord. Thank you, Gene and Hazel Slocum, of Redding. You two live what you preach.

When the counselors arrived at the jail, I was surprised when they didn't shove us around or beat us up. They were polite and even bought us a hamburger during the trip back to Preston.

# FIFTEEN

We spent the night in solitary. At 5 a.m., a counselor woke me up. He had me dress, then helped me to a waiting van and lifted me into it. Stubby was already there.

In the van they placed leg irons and belly chains around me. After they finished, Stubby asked what I thought was going on. I figured we would know before the day was through.

My foot looked like a medicine ball; I was in severe pain. The counselors ignored my request for medical attention but let us talk and smoke. One of the counselors even bought us a pack of cigarettes and a sandwich along the way, but they refused to tell us where we were going.

It was not a long drive. Then I saw a sight right out of the movies.

I saw high fences lined with towers where guards stood with rifles in their hands. Inside the fences were several buildings, each several stories high. Within a penned area, hundreds of men were milling about.

As I took all of this in, one of the counselors turned to me from the front seat. "Welcome to Deuels," he said.

I knew Deuels as a place where riots occurred and people died, where nearly every day someone was stabbed or badly beaten.

The gate swung open. A guard searched the van, looking under it and checking inside, too. He signaled to another guard who stood in the gun tower above us, and a second gate opened. The van pulled to the side of the inmate receiving and release building.

A guard appeared, unlocked a door and led us inside the building. There, I saw several more guards and some inmates standing around. They were all years order than us, and watched us intently as our chains were removed. We were ordered to strip off all our clothing.

As we stood there naked, the inmates moved closer toward us. A guard told Stubby, "Stand in the middle of the room, on that painted line."

Stubby walked there and stood still. The guard checked for possible contraband hidden in his armpits, ears, nose and mouth. He told Stubby to turn around, lift each foot and wiggle his toes. Then, the guard told him to bend over and spread the cheeks of his butt with his hands. Stubby bent over, and the inmates whistled and made cat calls. One of the guards laughed, "You boys'll have fun with this one."

Stubby and I were what is considered "choice" in prison. We were young, cute, and did not have much body hair.

I watched Stubby go through this humiliation. Knowing him as I did, I could tell he was ready to cry. I hoped he wouldn't. It would have been a serious mistake.

It was my turn. A guard noticed my injured foot. He told me to sit down on a bench, and searched me there. I could see the disappointment on the faces of the inmates who watched. I didn't put on a show for them.

We showered, had our hair cut, had mug shots taken and then dressed in prison issue. A medical assistant briefly examined me. My foot was X-rayed for the first time. The assistant found several fractures.

I needed a cast and had to stay in the hospital. Stubby was assigned to a cell by himself, in general population. Later, I found out that one of the guards who had searched us told the cellblock officer it was best to give Stubby his own cell.

My hospital stay was a drag. All I did for a week was lay in bed and stare at the ceiling. The cast drove me crazy. I was released just before the noon meal and placed in the same cell with Stubby. When I walked through the cellblock, hobbling on crutches, my gut tightened. All the inmates on the tiers stopped their conversations and stared at me. Some of them started smacking their lips, making kissing sounds. Others jeered. They all appeared to be at least 10 years older than me.

There were three tiers on the cellblock. The bottom tier had a full floor. The cells faced each other. A flight of stairs led up to the other tiers. The lighting was dingy, and the place had a filthy look about it, even though Deuels at that time was a newly built prison.

There were doors, instead of bars, on each cell. Each door had four small windows. Most were broken.

I saw my cell number and stepped inside. On the right was a steel toilet, with a sink attached on top of it. On the left were two metal bunk beds, each bolted to the wall. Encased in the back wall were several small windows, like the ones in the door.

Stubby was sitting on the lower bunk. When I shut the door behind me, he burst out bawling. He held me so tight that he almost had me crying, too. Something was wrong. I began to get a sick feeling in my stomach.

Stubby reached for a pack of cigarettes and gave me a smoke. I wondered where he'd gotten them, but I didn't ask.

Slowly, he began telling me that on his second day there, he had been taking a shower when several guys had beat him up. After that, they raped him repeatedly. Stubby said he had a daddy who was protecting him and giving him stuff from the inmates' store in exchange for sex.

I was able to reach the toilet before I started heaving. Stubby's words struck me like physical blows. First came pain, then came anger, knowing that someone had dared to rape my friend. Fear creeped in as well. From what I'd seen, most of the inmates were much older and bigger than us. Paso and Preston was kindergarten compared to the way things are done at Deuels.

Stubby cried himself out as all these thoughts came to me. I allowed my fear to sharpen my senses and not take control. A stupid act now, at Deuels, could cost us our lives. I was having serious doubts as to my ability to protect myself, much less the both of us. Still, I intended to do my best and not let him down.

We remained inside our cell all that day and did not go out to lunch or dinner. Stubby told me everything he'd seen, and I listened carefully. I searched for an answer, for a way out of a physical confrontation.

After dinner, the inmates in our cellblock returned. A big white guy, about 40 years old, came to the door of our cell and put his face in through the open frame of a broken window.

"Hey, Stubby," he said.

Stubby didn't answer. He remained seated on the bunk, watching him. The guy looked over at me.

"What's your problem?" he asked.

"I have no problem."

"Do you have a daddy yet?"

"I don't know what you're talking about."

"Who's punking you, boy?"

"I don't mess around that way."

The man called to some inmates, "Look in here at the new pretty boy." Then he looked in at me and said, "See you at shower time, pretty boy."

They left. "Those are the same guys who got me," Stubby said. "That one with the mouth is Porgy. He's my daddy."

I'd figured that. What I couldn't figure was why this was happening. I know now that sending kids to Deuels was the CYA's attempt to frighten children into discontinuing their rebellion. It was of no matter that we might be beaten, raped and possibly murdered. It was one hell of a way to correct mistakes.

That night, Stubby and I went to the shower room but did not shower. We remained fully clothed. We stood near a wall, in an area where we would not be out of view of the guard who sat at a desk next to the door of the cellblock entrance.

Inside the shower room, I attempted to talk with Porgy and his buddies, but they only had one thing on their minds. They knew we could not possibly win if we tried to fight them.

One of them pulled a shank, to intimidate us to go to the shower. Stubby took a step toward that area. I grabbed his arm and pulled him with me as I hobbled back to the cell.

It seemed to me the cons should have learned it was a mistake to scare someone so badly that the person becomes convinced he must act fast to avoid being killed. They also made a mistake not using the shank after pulling it, since the intended victim might well return to haunt them.

By the time we were locked inside our cell, I was shaking uncontrollably. I avoided letting Stubby know how frightened I was. I was sure these guys meant to kill us if we didn't do what they demanded.

We talked long into the night. I wanted to sleep with Stubby but figured he was through with all of that between us. But moments after I crawled in my bed, Stubby asked me to be with him. We needed solace and strength from each other.

After lying in bed for a while, mulling over my options, I decided to make a shank. I removed a bedspring, straightened it and sharpened it on the concrete floor. I tore several strips of cloth from a bedsheet and wrapped them around the spring to form a handle. By the time I fell asleep, I felt a little more secure, though not by much.

I woke several times throughout the night. I dressed an hour before breakfast. Stubby and I talked about what might await us that day. No doubt Porgy and his friends thought they'd scared the hell out of us. They were right, but there was no doubt we'd fight. If anything kicked off, we'd stand together and do the best we could.

I knew my cast had to go. Stubby helped me break it and take it off my leg. I took the shank from my pillow case and placed it in my waistband. My unbuttoned coat concealed the weapon but would allow me to get to it quickly, if I had to.

My hands were shaking, and I realized I had to calm myself. Anyone who saw me might assume that I was too scared to stand up to them. Stubby was not a good fighter. That worried me.

The guard opened the door, and my gut fluttered. Stubby and I looked at each other. I adjusted my coat, and we stepped out of the cell.

I was looking in every direction at once. I saw Porgy with about six other inmates, walking to a stairway that led from the second tier down to the first. They were looking at us. We walked down the long corridor, heading for the mess hall. I noticed that most of the younger inmates, those near our age, wore tight clothing. Their eyebrows had been trimmed, and some wore makeup. I wondered if they had tried to avoid doing those things, and why they had given up. Were our efforts going to do us any good?

No one bothered us by the time we got to the mess hall. Food was slopped on the metal trays by convicts assigned kitchen duty. The cons stared as we made our way to a table. We stood out like sissies in boys' town. They had seen Stubby for a whole week. That left me the star attraction, the new pretty boy on the block.

We had just begun to eat when Porgy and his gang walked over.

"You're at my table," Porgy said, keeping an eye on me. "Find another one." He pointed to Stubby. "But you stay."

I stood and looked at Stubby, saying, "Let's find another table."

Stubby hesitated, then stood.

"Sit your punk ass down!" shouted Porgy.

Ignoring him, we took off with our trays. The noise was way down as everyone looked on, watching the drama unfold. We won the first round. There was no reason to fear a physical confrontation at the moment. There were too many guards nearby.

After eating, we dumped our trays and utensils into a big washpan, but hung onto our steel knives, concealing them inside my waistband, next to my shank.

Leaving the mess hall, I was aware Porgy and his buddies were following us down the hall. Porgy called to Stubby, who turned around. He should have ignored him. Instead, he froze. I saw the fear in his eyes, which got me scared, too.

At the moment, I was interested only in reaching the safety of our cell and sharpening the two knives. They would serve us better than the bed spring.

I told Stubby to move his butt, but he seemed to freeze. I saw his fear, which scared me. I fought to regain control, using my fear to see me through and keep us both alive.

Porgy's group was trying to encircle us. I took Stubby by his arm and pulled him with me so our backs were to the wall, keeping anyone from getting behind us.

Porgy did all the talking. He tried to convince me that Stubby belonged to him. He said I would have to choose one of his friends to be my daddy.

"If you don't choose," he said, "the choice will be made for you."

Suddenly, a con sucker-punched me. I had done it again. I was concentrating on Porgy and had taken my attention away from the others. The blow landed on my nose, and my head slammed against the wall. I would have passed out, had someone not kicked me in the head, which somehow brought me back to my senses.

I dove into one of them, pulling my weapon. Someone yelled, "Look out! He's got a shank!" Everyone backed away from me as I stood there holding the shank and wiping blood from my eyes.

The hall was quiet as church. Some inmate said, "We'll deal with you later." I charged at him. He jumped back out of range. Porgy and the others took off.

An older man, about 60 years old, approached us.

"Kid," he said, "you got balls. You need help? You got it. Meet me in the big yard after the noon meal."

This was totally out of left field. I hadn't been looking for help in such a place. When we got back to our cell, I didn't get on Stubby's case. I understood why he froze. We sat on the concrete floor, working together to sharpen the knives I'd ripped off. We had them ready before lunch. I asked Stubby, "Will you be able to use it if the situation calls for it? I need to be sure so I know what I'm dealing with."

His answer was honest: "I'm not sure." Nothing I could say in the short time before we had yard call would make a bit of difference.

Skipping lunch, we walked straight to the yard. I wondered why the old con offered his help. Was he trying to run a game on us? I couldn't trust his motives, but needed his help badly if he was for real.

We saw him walking toward us with about 20 other inmates. Again, I got a sick feeling. Maybe they were coming in force to get what a few had not been able to do.

The old man put out his hand. "My name's Grumpy."

We shook hands.

"What do you want from us?" I asked.

He studied my face for a moment, then smiled. "Kid, I can help you out, but we've got a couple of problems. First, I'm not trying to get into your pants or your friend's. My friends ain't either. I don't like people getting beat up and raped, like your sidekick here. Besides, looks to me like you've got the balls to fight back. If you hadn't shown me that, we wouldn't be here now."

One of the problems, he said, was that Stubby had allowed Porgy to become his daddy. Had Stubby fought back or killed Porgy after it happened, Grumpy and his bunch could have helped. But now, the only way Stubby could get out of the situation with Porgy was if he decided to be my punk.

"Then and only then will me and my friends here back you up in your effort to protect yourselves," Grumpy said.

The law of the jungle is, partners protect one another, as well as their partners' punks.

Grumpy's words disturbed me. Stubby was no jailhouse sissy, and I had no desire to be his daddy. I only wanted to be his friend and to be there when he needed me.

The second problem, Grumpy said, was Porgy. The issue was far from over. "In fact, it's just beginning. He has to make a move on you to save face. You pulled a shank and tried to use it. He walked away. If he doesn't do anything to get Stubby away from you, he'll lose respect. You've got to kill him."

Grumpy and his clique would stand with me against Porgy's friends if they tried to avenge his death. That was the code among convicts.

Stubby resolved the first problem. He said it would be better if he was known as my punk. He said it would not bother him, as long as no one else was doing anything to him, and as long as we were still friends and all else was just show. That made sense to me. It was the only solution we had. I agreed to it, although it left a bad taste in my mouth.

I asked Grumpy how I was supposed to get Porgy without his friends stopping me or the guards seeing me do it. He told me there were ways to trick Porgy into going to an area where I would be waiting. No one else would be around. By the time it was announced over the speaker system that the yard was closing, everything had been worked out.

Back at the cell, Stubby trimmed his eyebrows and used a pencil to put eyeliner on. Watching him, I felt totally depressed, like Stubby had left and a stranger had taken his place. He looked just like a girl. I hated it. Until those creeps had raped him, Stubby had never done anything with anybody, except me. That thought made it easy for me to want to kill Porgy.

That night, as we laid together, we discussed what I had to do to Porgy. Stubby argued that it would be better if we went to protective custody. He was more afraid for me than he was for himself. If we stayed out of trouble and managed to stay alive, we both knew we'd be released in a few months. Protective custody was the last place I wanted to be.

The next morning, I never had a chance to get to Porgy. Walking down the hallway toward the mess hall, someone shoved Stubby aside and several convicts were suddenly stabbing me.

"Guards coming!" someone yelled.

I heard a whistle. Somehow, I put my back to the wall. I saw Stubby and several other convicts lying face down on the concrete. Guards were handcuffing them. Stubby was yelling.

I looked down. My jacket was soaked with blood. I tried to say something but couldn't speak. My hand brushed against a hard object protruding from my neck. It was the handle of an ice pick.

I woke in a hospital outside the prison walls. I was lucky. The ice picks poked holes in me without damaging vital spots. Had they been blades, I wouldn't have made it. The pick that had been left in my throat entered at the side and exited through the back.

There were three other major punctures: Two in my back and one on the upper left side of my chest. I had a razor cut on my left side and several on my chest that looked worse than they really were. It took several hundred sutures to close all the wounds.

After a couple of days in the hospital, I was taken back to Deuels and admitted to the infirmary. Though the staff asked me a lot of questions, I intended to deal with the assailants myself after I returned to the cellblock.

I learned Stubby was confined to solitary confinement, along with several other inmates who were under investigation. I assured staff that Stubby had nothing to do with the stabbing.

After six days in the infirmary I was discharged to administrative segregation, i.e., protective custody.

I argued against being placed there. No one listened, so I set fire to my bed sheets. They promptly put me in solitary. There, I found Stubby, Porgy and a few of his friends. To my surprise, Grumpy was there, too.

Stubby and I yelled back and forth. I assured him, in my sandpaper voice, that everything was fine. Grumpy yelled to be careful with what I said, since guards listened to the conversations. Soon I received a small bundle called a "kite" from the tier porter. Wrapped in a note were smokes and matches. The note was from Grumpy, who wanted to know what the guards had said. He wrote he had been on his way to meet me at the entrance of the chow hall when I was jumped. He and two of his partners had gotten into it, but I had already been hit. Guards had grabbed them when they tried to get away from the area.

I wrote back to Grumpy, answering his questions. Then I got a kite from Porgy, and I let him know that I hadn't snitched. I added that he and I would talk when we got out of the hole. Grumpy wrote me later that evening that all of us would be in the segregation yard together for an hour each morning.

The next morning, after breakfast in our cells, we were let out one at a time, searched, then placed in the exercise yard. Stubby, Grumpy and a couple of other convicts were waiting right outside the door for me. Porgy and his pals were standing across the yard, watching me as I walked over to Stubby and shook his hand.

Putting us together in the yard was an obvious set up. The guards wanted things to hit the fan so they could finger my attacker. I knew what they were up to, but I knew I'd still go after Porgy before the hour was up.

The yard was only about 20 feet by 20 feet, enclosed by buildings on three sides. On the fourth was a fence, topped with barbed wire. Atop one of the buildings was a gun tower. I looked up and saw a guard who didn't look too interested in what went on below him.

When I told Grumpy that I was going after Porgy, he looked at me for a moment, then smiled. "You're going to make out all right, kid."

There were no weapons. It had to be a good old-fashioned street fight. Porgy said, "You're crazy to start something with that gun above us."

Grumpy replied, "You're stupid for what you did out on the hallway."

Those words were no sooner out of his mouth than we were all fighting, even Stubby.

It was understood that Porgy belonged to me. I expected to get my butt kicked, and Porgy didn't disappoint me. I tripped, and someone kicked me on the rib cage, where I had just been sewn up. That hurt like crazy. I got to my feet in time for Porgy to split open the skin above my eye. I fell back against the fence as he came at me. I kicked him hard where it counted.

The kick doubled him over. I kicked out again, missing his head by inches. He jumped on top of me, pinned me, then smashed me in the face several times before someone pulled him off me.

A shot rang out and whistles blew. "Break it up!" the guards shouted. We kept on fighting until another shot was fired. We split into two groups and stood against a wall.

"I shoot the next man who moves!" yelled the guard in the tower.

Stubby was bleeding badly from cuts on his face. I lost my composure and ran at Porgy, who was standing pressed against the fence. The guard in the tower fired another shot.

I didn't feel the bullet as it entered my body. I tried to get up, but my legs wouldn't respond. Stubby loomed over me for a moment. I watched two guards grab him.

"Man down!" someone yelled. "Get the stretcher!"

Soon there were more guards in that small yard than I thought worked the entire joint. Some began to handcuff the inmates. Others kneeled over me.

"My God," one said. "He's just a baby."

"Yep, and his luck sure sucks."

"Looks like he got hit in his leg and left side," someone said.

As it turned out, the bullet hit my leg. My side was bleeding badly from a reopened wound. I heard Stubby, sobbing, begging for them to help me as he was being led from the yard.

"How bad am I hurt?" I asked a guard.

He looked away from me without saying a word. Suddenly, I began to fall into shock. Someone beside me was telling me to stay awake, that I would be all right and should hang on. Whoever talked to me kept me awake and conscious.

Guards lifted me onto the stretcher and carried me into the segregation area. On the way there, some guys yelled to me from their cells.

"Hang in there."

"You'll be all right."

Grumpy shouted, "If you die, kid, someone else will, too."

The guards ran the stretcher to an awaiting ambulance. The medics, checking me over, told me I was going to be fine. I felt relieved when they told me I had only been shot in the leg.

At the hospital, the same doctor who had treated my stab wounds greeted me. "What the hell are they doing to you kids in there?" he asked.

Once out of surgery, the doctor said he had removed the bullet and assured me that there should be no complications. He wanted to know how I had ended up in prison. I shared with him a little bit about my life, and about Stubby's, too. His interest in me caused us to be released from prison nine weeks later.

Back at prison after two days in the hospital, I was sent to solitary since I refused to go to the infirmary. All of us involved in the fight were taken before a disciplinary committee. We were all given 30 days in the hole and were exercised in two separate groups during that time; Porgy and his bunch, then Stubby, me, Grumpy and our other new friends. No one was ever charged with stabbing me, and no one would say who started the fight. Nobody ratted, so that was the end of it for the time being.

When the 30 days were completed, everyone except Stubby and me were returned to the main population. We raised hell about it, unaware that the doctor and his friends were helping us on the outside. We were held in the hole until the parole board interviewed us and considered us for release.

One day, without warning, a couple of guards took us before the board. They told us we would be released. I was to go home to my family in Redding. Stubby was to go back to a father who cared nothing about him.

Two days later, after the cast was removed from my leg, Stubby and I were given a set of street clothes and driven to the bus depot in Tracy. While we waited for our separate buses with guards standing nearby, we said goodbye. It was a very difficult moment. We made hell bearable for one another.

We exchanged phone numbers, then hugged each other tightly. We separated with tears in our eyes. It was the closest I had ever come to crying.

My bus arrived first. I looked out the window at Stubby walking alongside the bus as it pulled out of the station. The last I saw of my friend, he stood waving as the bus turned the corner. Then I couldn't see him any more.

What was it like to be free after all those years? There are no words. I really knew nothing about the world my bus was entering into. I hadn't seen it since I was very young.

In Redding, my parents were waiting for me. Mom and Dad

rushed to greet me. They hugged me so tight I could hardly breathe. Dad took a paper sack that contained all of my worldly possessions and led me to the car.

We stopped for something to eat. For the first time in my life, I ate inside a restaurant.

When we got home, I asked if we could just walk around the property instead of going inside the house. I stripped off my clothes to my underwear and swam in the creek. Mom and Dad stood at the edge and watched.

It was near dark when I came out of the water. I noticed them both staring at my upper body. I glanced down to see what they were looking at. Then I realized the purple and red scars had drawn their attention. Dad started to ask something, but I turned away. He never finished the sentence.

Back at the house, I dialed the number Stubby had given me. Whoever answered said Stubby wasn't there. I called back the next day and learned he had not been on the bus when it arrived.

I haven't heard from Stubby since that day at the bus depot. I've always asked myself why he never called me. I wonder if he's still alive and, if so, what he's done with his life. If you ever read this, Stubby, I love you, my friend. I would like to hear from you.

# SIXTEEN

I do not know why it was decided I would go live with Danny and his wife. I'm sure much of it had to do with Mom and Dad trying to make me happy. There was so much about me they didn't understand. How could they? I didn't know what was driving me myself.

Nothing went right those three days I stayed with Danny and Rita, in Reseda. I heard them discussing me a couple of times. Once, I heard Rita say she was frightened of me living in the same house.

Danny told me he thought it best if I moved to a motel. He paid for a room, and I became very lonely. Afraid might be a better word. I knew nothing about living on my own. I couldn't find a job. I walked around for hours doing nothing, not wanting to be there.

I stole a car and headed for wherever the road went. I was arrested in Arizona on a federal charge of Dire Act, taking a stolen car across a state line. I had an identification card on me that was stolen, too. As unlikely as it seems, I convinced FBI agents that I was a 32-year-old named Whyne Edgar Watkins. I was 17 and looked younger.

In Tucson, I pleaded guilty and was sentenced to five years in federal prison. I was transported to the California federal prison, in Lompoc.

On my arrival, one of the guards asked if I preferred to be locked away from the other prisoners. He honored my request to be placed in general population. My fellow convicts instinctively knew I was not even 18 — the minimum age — let alone 32.

No doubt what saved me a lot of misery and physical abuse was the fact that there were many guys inside that prison who had children. In those days, a young man would be assisted by the older convicts to be respected and be allowed to do his own time. That is, unless he wasn't a snitch or a child molester.

Today is different. Unless he's an unusually violent person, a young man will become somebody's punk in a matter of days. If considered pretty, a young con has two choices: Become a punk or die.

At Lompoc, a couple of older inmates took me under their wings. For a while, no one made any sexual advances toward me, although many considered me as I walked by. Wherever I went, one of the two cons always remained by my side. I knew everyone thought I was a punk and was receiving protection from these two guys in return for sex.

One con named George persisted in sending me love letters, telling me he'd make a good husband and let no one harm me. I didn't tip off my partners, because I knew they might kill the guy. As it turned out, my silence was a serious mistake.

My cell partner, Shawn, had just stepped outside onto the tier when I heard the sound of shuffling feet and flesh hitting flesh. I stuck my head out of the cell and saw Shawn getting cut by George, who had a shank in his hand.

In a second, I reached under Shawn's mattress, where he kept a two foot length of steel pipe. I ran from the cell and brought the pipe down on George's head.

Unaware of what had put him on the floor, George went down. Shawn yelled to me, "Get in the cell!"

I turned to run as I heard a whistle blow. Guards! Shawn rolled George over the rail. I stood there, stunned, watching George fall 12 feet and hit the first tier's concrete floor.

I still had the bloody pipe in my hand. Blood was also splattered all over my shirt. It was just beginning to dawn on me that we had killed someone.

"Throw the weapon out of the cell!" a guard yelled.

I looked at Shawn, sitting on the bottom bunk. He looked at me with sort of a smile. I didn't respond quickly enough for the guard, who shot me with a 12-gauge tear gas gun. I fell back against the toilet. They slammed our door shut.

The other inmates on the cellblock began to yell. Soon, the entire place became dense with smoke from the fires they lit.

The inmates threw bars of soap and hidden weapons at the guards, who left the tier to regroup. It was now a full-scale riot. Everybody was throwing stashed weapons from their cells, anticipating the lockdown and search.

In the melee, Shawn and I seized the chance to rid ourselves of weapons. We wiped the pipe clean, and tossed it on the tier.

The guards returned in riot gear. Walking from one cell to the next, they hosed water into the cells, soaking every convict and putting out fires on the tiers.

Once the guards had regained control, Shawn and I were ordered back up to the bars. They handcuffed us before opening the door.

They escorted us to the warden's office, where we learned George was still alive but appeared to have a broken back and other undetermined injuries.

Two guards took Shawn from the office. I was left alone with the warden and a captain.

"Come clean, kid," the captain said. "We know it's all Shawn's fault. You're just a pawn in the whole matter."

I sat there while they played good-guy, bad-guy with me. When they tired of the game, two guards escorted me to solitary and placed me two cells away from Shawn.

Shawn sent a kite telling me his back had been stitched up. The guard who escorted him to the hole said George would probably die. Shawn said if George died, he intended to tell the warden it was his fault.

For the first time, I told Shawn I was only 17 years old and, if George died, I'd say I hit George because he tried to rape me. Shawn got angry with me. He said he figured I was lying about my age, but not by so many years.

We were in the hole nearly two months before the disciplinary committee told us George would live. They sentenced us to another 90 days in solitary.

The day after the hearing, I suffered an appendicitis attack, and underwent surgery. Days after the operation, the captain walked to my hospital cell and asked if it was true I was only 17.

He handed me a note from Shawn that said he couldn't see me remaining at Lompoc and was sorry for snitching.

I refused to talk to the captain. He returned with Shawn, who told me they were sending him to Alcatraz, and was worried I wouldn't survive alone because George had friends in Lompoc. He was right.

The FBI contacted my parents. They confirmed I was 17.

There was quite an uproar about that. Someone had made the mistake of not checking my fingerprints. Reform groups had a field day attacking the feds for sending a minor to a federal prison. They even circulated my picture. On the pamphlet was the question, "Does this child look 32 years old?" I looked more like 12.

Dad came to pick me up. While several guards looked on, Dad tried to say something but burst into tears. I'd never seen him cry before.

I hurt for Dad as he cried, but was unable to express my feelings or show the emotion I felt.

To survive, children who are locked away must learn to become the very best of actors. But a time comes in the incarcerated boy's life when the act becomes so real that he forgets who and what he really is.

Dad is dead now. I never had the chance to say that I love him very much and am sorry for the pain I caused him. I do so now, and pray he is watching over me.

I will take to the grave the pain I feel for the grief I caused Mom and Dad. It is something that cannot be forgotten.

# EPILOGUE

The book ends, but the story does not. My life became uncontrollable. I have served most of my life in prison.

I've served time at San Quentin, Vacaville, Oregon State Penitentiary, Washington State Penitentiary, Lompoc Federal Prison and Folsom State Prison, where I am now writing a book about my adult life.

My crimes have ranged from stealing cars to murder and everything in between. I once called Charles Manson my friend. Gary Gilmore and I went through the system together in Oregon. George Jackson and some of his friends nearly stabbed me to death, just prior to Jackson's murder by guards during a bloody escape attempt at San Quentin. For 16 years, I was involved with a group of white supremacists who were and are involved in organized crime nationwide, both in and out of prison.

I have corresponded with incarcerated children in New York, Florida, Texas, Oregon, New Mexico, Kansas, Georgia, Oklahoma, California and Washington. Nothing has changed since I spent my years in CYA, other than the sophistication level of the abuses — which makes them even more difficult to expose and prove.

There is nothing anyone can do for me now. But I hope that I have convinced people with this book that drastic changes must be made within the juvenile correctional system.

It is your system. You have the power to control what happens to the children. If you put this book aside and neglect to seek a way to help the childen, then I've failed.

I would like to close this story in the memory of an 11-year-old boy who killed himself a short while ago. He had been incarcerated several times, for many reasons. Recently, his older brother wrote to me. I will share the letter with you here.

Dear Dwight,

I'm sorry to tell you that Lyle killed himself on July 18. He left a note that said he didn't want to be bothered any more by Mr. Forest. I am sending you a letter he wrote for you just before he died. I hope you will not be upset as I tell you I read it. No one else knows about it.

As you can see, Lyle died because Mr. Forest had been sexually molesting him since Lyle was 6. He never told anyone that I know of.

I am 20 years old and went through a similar situation with this same man and never told anyone until now.

Dwight, Lyle talked about you a lot. I know he loved you very much. I promise you that I will get even with Mr. Forest for what he has done.

Thank you for caring for my brother. Until you came along when he was in juvenile, I was his only pal.

Goodbye,
Wes

The letter above appears exactly as it was written, except that I changed the names and used the word "juvenile" in place of the institution named in the letter. A little later, Wes got even with Mr. Forest.

The following is the letter Lyle wrote to me. It appears exactly as he sent it.

Dear Dwight,

Four a long tyme, I want to have sumone I can talk to but I no if I told about Mr. Forrest no buddy wood want me any mor. Mr. Forrest has been do ing things tyme sence I was 6. He made me do nastie things. I hope you will still lyke me becase I luv you a lot. Plese don't bee mad at me.

    your pal,
    Lyle

What else can I say? Lyle and Wes said it all. Readers can contact me at this address:

Dwight E. Abbott
C-92115
P.O. Box 29
Represa, CA. 95671

**The View from Solitary,
El Paso de Robles School for Boys**

# America's Incarcerated Children Today

## Report by Jack Carter

Do the kinds of abuses described in this book occur today within our juvenile correctional institutions?

No precise figure can be calculated, but the answer is clear. A vast number of our incarcerated children are being abused — physically, emotionally and sexually.

According to the 1990 Universal Almanac , a full 9 percent of the America's 878,909 inmates are children. Some of those prisoners are as young as 5 years old.

In a July 1986 case study, researchers with the University of California, Los Angeles, determined that 53 percent of the female wards interviewed said they had been physically and/or sexually abused while incarcerated; 26 percent of the male inmates surveyed had been physically and/or sexually abused while incarcerated. It should be kept in mind that only a percentage of abused children will ever admit it their victimization to anyone.

In an October 1988 study, researchers with the New York University School of Medicine found that five of the 14 juvenile offenders currently held on American death rows said they had been sexually abused by relatives and/or staff members at their juvenile correctional institutions. Twelve of the 14 offenders said they had been brutally beaten with whips and/or belts. All 14 had suffered serious head injuries as children. "Criminal acts committed by children [are] the result of a festering wound," one researcher concluded.

In an August 1989 investigation of the Western New York Children's Psychiatric Center by a New York state commission, investigators found 64 separate incidents of adult staff members sexually abusing the center's juvenile wards. According to the report, sexual abuse between wards and staff was overlooked and was even encouraged between the children as "normal behavior."

Despite all the studies and investigations, apologists for the juvenile correctional system continue to deny that abuses occur. Beyond denial and ignorance, there exists the offensive belief that a beaten or raped child is "getting his due" for committing a crime. Swift and severe punishment, some contend, is the best and only way to manage troubled youth.

Unfortunately, this view is often held by the people charged with the operation of the juvenile system itself.

With the publication of this book, we wanted to bring attention to the children, who for reasons of their own, remain silent in the face of their suffering.

Dwight E. Abbott is one of hundreds of thousands of people who has experienced the kinds of abuses described in this book. Some of the other victims include today's most notorious criminals.

Charles Manson's childhood was similar to Abbott's. At 14, Manson became a ward of the state of Indiana and was sent to the Indiana Boys School, in Plainfield. Within two days of his arrival, Manson was gang raped by a group of older wards. Guards beat Manson daily with a wooden paddle and a leather strap. "[We would] take him out in the corn field and beat the piss out of him," said one former administrator.

Over the next 22 years, 12 other such institutions were home to Manson, each being one step closer to the penitentiary cell where he now resides.

Gary Gilmore, who attained notoriety after killing a gas station attendant and then demanding his own execution, was also a victim of childhood abuse. An older male relative frequently molested Gilmore when he was a child, a fact not reported in Norman Mailer's biography, The Executioner's Song. At 14, Gilmore was sent to a Portland reform school. Eighteen of the next 22 years of his life were spent in and out of juvenile facilities and adult prisons.

In April 1990, Robert Alton Harris nearly became the first murderer in 23 years to be executed in California. The day Harris was born, his father repeatedly kicked his mother in the abdomen. She began to hemorrhage, and Harris was born three months premature. Both parents beat him daily; the boy could not walk into a room without someone punching him.

From age 6 through adolescence, Harris took every kind of drug imaginable. For a hobby, he killed neighborhood pets. Later, he graduated to killing people.

After hearing Dwight Abbott's powerful and troubling life story, I felt a responsibility to substantiate its almost inconceivable claims.

I contacted officials with the California Youth Authority and stated my intention to tour as many of its juvenile institutions as possible. I received permission to visit three of them, then scheduled my visits in the order in which Abbott was incarcerated.

Touring the facilities in sequence offered observations of the youthful offenders' progression from small-time hoods, picked up for petty thefts or drugs, to the hardcore "gladiator," ready for California's adult facilities.

"Some of these wards," said one CYA official, "will be dependent on the state for the rest of their lives."

I began the investigation with a tour of the Fred C. Nelles School, in Whittier, where Abbott had been sent after escaping from the state mental hospital at Camarillo.

Nelles functions today as a secondary phase detention center, incarcerating youths who have had problems adjusting to Los Angeles County Juvenile Hall, youth camps and foster homes.

Outside the main gate at Nelles, tall evergreens hide from view thousands of yards of razor wire coiled atop the facility's fence.

Flatbed trucks drive through a gate opening between two chain-link fences. Wards wearing blue jeans and white T-shirts are transported to work details outside the institution.

A guard seated inside the security and admissions building at the front of the facility uses switches to control the electric gates.

The last flatbed filled with wards leaves the compound; the gates close slowly behind it.

Inside the compound, two dozen uniformed guards stand about in groups. The guards are linked to the facility's communications center by walkie-talkie, which blare a garbled message.

"Wards spotted near the corner of Broadway and Bexley..."

Had there been an escape attempt?

A public relations officer arrives. Introductions are made. I ask the officer when the last escape occurred at Nelles.

"Today," the officer replies. "Two."

Nelles' top administrators offer sociological breakdowns of their wards: 49 percent are black and Hispanic, 49 percent are white, and 2 percent are Asian. Wards face problems, they say, of drug and alcohol abuse, single-parent and dysfunctional families, and peer pressures that plague the lower economic strata.

Administrators speak highly of Nelles' various programs, designed to assimilate wards to the outside world, "a place where they have failed," one adds. Nelles' programs stress responsibility, punctuality and proper social behavior.

Administrators are proud of a program called "Free Venture," in which Nelles' most mature wards package plastic spoons and napkins for a fast-food restaurant chain. Free Venture includes a forced savings program, to teach budgeting and fiscal responsibility.

Drug and alcohol rehabilitation is another priority program. "I can count on two fingers the number of wards who come in here and didn't do drugs," says one counselor. Basic education, community service and public restitution round out the rest of the facility's programs, all funded by state tax dollars. "I tell people, 'Come visit us,'" says one administrator. "'Come see what your tax money's doing.' Sometimes they do."

While each of these programs aim to curb an admitted 51 percent recidivism rate, questions remain concerning the treatment of wards during their incarcerations within the CYA.

A counselor at Nelles speaks quietly from inside a caged office overlooking a dormitory. Forty boys are lying on their bunks during an afternoon rest period.

"At night, when only one counselor is on [duty] is when the problems occur," the counselor says. "That's when we have the homosexual acts, the fighting, the drug use. The kids know when the counselor's here, and they know when he's gone to check on another dorm. [The counselor] can't be everywhere at once."

When questioned about abuse by staff members, the counselor says, "There are forms the ward can file. The ward does have recourse, if he proves it's true."

Are the wards likely to report the crime, and if they do, who will the administration be more apt to believe, a fellow employee or a possibly vengeful youth?

"I don't know," the counselor admits. "I guess it depends on the situation."

Cover-ups do occur within the system. Consider the case of former Superior Court Judge Gary Little, of Seattle. On Oct. 14, 1986, the *Seattle Times* reported that the Washington State Commission on Judicial Conduct had failed in 1984 to discipline Judge Little after board members learned that the judge indulged in many out-of-court contacts with male juvenile offenders.

According to the report, Little preferred to make sexual advances toward "slender, blond, teenaged boys" who had been sent before his court since 1964. In exchange for reduced sentences, Little demanded "often violent homosexual sex acts" with the juveniles. The morning the *Times* published the story, Little was found dead inside his chambers, killed by a self-inflicted gunshot.

Washington State's Judicial Board — established to monitor the court's authority over juveniles — knew of Little's improprieties for more than 10 years and did not act to rectify the problem, the *Times* reported.

Protected by the shroud of secrecy and cronyism, the truth is hard to uncover. It is not known how many other judges, administrators and counselors use their authority to abuse incarcerated children.

Standing in a recreation yard at Nelles, near a doorway to one dormitory, a counselor points to a high wall across the yard.

"That's what the boys call 'Madison Square Garden,'" he says. "That's where they take the new kids and work them over. Because of the angle [from the doorway], it's hard to see anything going on. Most of the wards are real cool about it, too. We don't know what's happened until the kid comes back in, beat to hell."

As when Abbott spent his time at Nelles, cliques, tips and other social pecking orders exist today, counselors say. The wards separate themselves first by race, then by his level of expertise at physical intimidation.

In the recent past, juvenile clique leaders at Nelles were allowed weekend furloughs to reward them for keeping their groups in line. "It made our job easier," explains the counselor. Those furloughs were stopped, however, when some of the group leaders began to overstay their furloughs or simply flee the area.

"They enjoy getting out, but they don't like to be seen as helping the Man," the counselor says. "That's perceived as being soft. Being hard means splitting when you get the chance. And some of them did."

Just outside the security and admissions building, several guards discuss the ongoing search for the two escaped wards. They await the return of the first contingent of guards, so they can fan out and catch the boys. Squeezed in a huddle like a junior varsity football squad, they settle upon a plan, then stride to their vans and squad cars.

A middle-aged maintenance worker sweeping nearby shakes his head. "Sure hope they don't find them," he says.

I ask him why.

The worker keeps sweeping. "Because they'll kick their asses, man. They'll kick their asses good."

Moments later, a call comes out over a walkie-talkie. The first search team found the escaped wards in a park, half a mile from Nelles.

The guards shout their approval of the news.

The escapees will soon be seated inside one of Nelles' solitary confinement cells — although administrators insist that those cells don't exist.

"What we have is an adjustment cottage," one says. "That's where the [wards with] behavioral problems are housed."

Nelles' "adjustment cottage" consists of individual concrete cells lined up along two separate hallways. The wards are allowed out of their cells one hour each day, as required by state law. Sentences to the cottage vary from four to nine months.

A counselor says wards are "dropped back [in sentencing], any time they mess up on the unit. The average stay is five months, although some kids stay longer because they act up longer."

I step inside one of the cells inside the cottage and measure off three short paces long, by two short paces wide. The cell is furnished with a steel commode and attached sink. Staff observes the prisoner through a small window within the steel door. A guard seated inside the cottage's main office monitors a ward's every move via a video camera.

A steel bed is bolted to the concrete wall. One wool blanket and a gray sheet are tucked under the edges of a thin mattress. To the left of the bed is a window. Light might leak into the cells if it weren't for the steel bars, wire mesh and caked-on dirt. Overhead, mounted inside a screened cage too far off the ground for anyone to reach, is a bare shining lightbulb.

I request that a guard leave me alone inside the cell.

He shuts the door, locking me in.

Standing inside, I realize there is little to see, do, or hear. There is an occasional noise from an adjacent cell; mostly, there is complete stillness and unnerving sensory deprivation.

A few moments pass. It becomes apparent that seeing a face — any face — at the door's window would be a welcome respite to the cell's emptiness. It is easy to see how feelings of hopelessness, despair and rage could quickly manifest themselves here within the mind and soul of the youthful offender.

It's cool inside the cell. Even wearing an undershirt, a long-sleeved shirt and a light jacket, I am cold. A ward locked inside this same cell for four to nine months wears a T-shirt and underwear.

The guard opens the door, and I step into the hallway. I ask him if the cells are kept cool to keep the level of activity down.

"I never heard a complaint," he says, walking down the hall.

In the hallway, another guard who's worked at Nelles for 25 years says the institution has gone through "several phases" of rehabilitation practices.

"When I began, we had a strong-arm policy," he says. "That was 1965."

I ask him to clarify "strong-arm."

"That means, more or less, you do whatever it takes to keep the boys in line."

He pauses for a moment, then continues.

"Next, in the early 1970s, we developed a therapeutic treatment program. Tried to get inside their heads. In the early 1980s, we had a point system, which awarded good behavior with points. You add up your points and get yourself back on the dorm. You lose points, you stay in the cottage. We don't use that now."

I ask him what kind of program Nelles has now, for wards sentenced to the adjustment cottage. He ponders that for a moment. Another guard passes by in the hallway, and the first guard jabs the other in the side.

"Hey, what kind of program we got now?" he asks.

The guard looks at him, shrugs his shoulders and continues walking down the hallway.

"Well," he says, scratching his head for effect, "I call it reality therapy. It's specialized, intensive therapy. You still see some of the other programs, too"

"Like strong-arm?"

"Well, only if a kid's acting up."

I describe for him Abbott's recollection of how he and others had to sit and stare at a dot on the wall for hours each day.

"I've heard of that, yes," the guard says. "But we don't do that now."

El Paso de Robles School, in Paso Robles, is what the CYA calls a midrange facility. At Paso, the Authority's juvenile offenders are introduced to an even more disciplined environment.

Paso receives wards who have been committed from courts throughout the state; 60 percent come from the Los Angeles area alone. Ethnically, 50 percent are black, 30 percent Hispanic, 13 percent white and lesser percentages are Asian and American Indian.

Juveniles are incarcerated at Paso for crimes ranging from burglary to murder. The wards here are considered violent and dangerous. Guards carry Mace, tear gas and handcuffs. They are in constant walkie-talkie communication with the facility's main security center, located inside a tower east of the dormitories.

The solitary confinement unit houses wards who attempt escapes, are involved in fights, or who steal or vandalize state property. If administrators cannot contain a more combative and violent ward, they generally transfer him further along the line, to the Preston School of Industry. "Preston has individual rooms there," says one Paso staff member. "We don't."

Escorted by a guard and a counselor, I tour some of the individual solitary confinement cells which Paso "doesn't have." I photograph the interiors of the cells while the men wait for me in the hallway.

Like the solitary cells at Nelles, most of Paso's are occupied. I look through the dirty windows on the steel doors and see wards laying on their beds, staring at the walls and through mesh-covered windows.

I ask to speak with one of the wards.

"You can't," the guard says. "It's policy."

I ask the guard about the existence of physical or sexual abuse. The counselor cuts in, "When there is a problem with, say, a stronger ward preying on a weaker one — for sexual purposes or for simply proving superiority — staff investigates the matter."

"To see if it's true," adds the guard.

"When there is an instance of sexual abuse, we take the

offender out and prosecute. If convicted of that crime, he is sent to state prison."

Since 1985, through use of district attorneys and the state's superior courts, Paso administrators have sent 12 juvenile wards to state prisons. Most were convicted of sodomy and oral copulation. In addition, staff says, there have been several accusations of coercion to perform a sexual act.

The Preston School of Industry, in Ione, holds California Youth Authority's oldest and most hardened wards. Preston is known as the end of the line. Mere mention of the name instills fear into the state's wards.

Sixty percent of the boys incarcerated there are remanded from one of the state's superior courts. The rest arrive from juvenile courts and CYA facilities throughout the system.

Overlooking the current Preston facility is the original, Romanesque structure known as "the castle," built in 1894. The first wards to be incarcerated there were seven juvenile inmates from San Quentin. They arrived at Preston on a hot July morning, handcuffed together inside a horse-drawn buckboard.

In 1894, Preston was known as a hell hole. A hundred years later, that perception has not changed.

Preston's solitary-confinement unit, called Tamarack, is located within the walls of an old, musty building. Sixty-four individual cells line the building's two main hallways. The red tiled floor has the same polished surface on which Abbott said he saw his reflection.

"Tamarack is the end of the road," says a staff member, walking beside me. "After this comes the state pen."

Most of the wards here will spend from four to nine months inside these cells, staring at the walls, shouting to other prisoners, trying to break the silence before the silence breaks them. They are fed from trays pushed through a slot in their doors, like zoo animals. For one hour each day, the wards are let out of their cells and are led into a caged enclosure at the side of the building. There, they pace or sit on the ground.

The staff member finds an unoccupied cell and unlocks the door. I step in and take a photograph.

The cell stinks horribly. It is in worse condition than those at Nelles or Paso. Graffiti and swastikas cover these walls: "Tin Man," "CCC" and "So Cal Peck." Pressed into the tiny holes of a thick wire mesh that cover the cell's window are similar messages, spelled with balls of tissue paper.

In the hallway outside, I ask the staff member about the abuses at Preston and throughout the CYA.

"[Critics of the CYA] don't talk about our programs or the rapport we establish with some of the wards," he says. "I admit there is sexual and physical abuse, and there are ways to reduce that. One [way] is to separate your stronger from your weaker wards, which we try to do. But keep in mind, you have a pecking order in any group, whether it's comprised of all your toughest wards or all your smallest and weakest. They act out their aggressions. That's one of the reasons they're here."

He acknowledges the presence of cliques. "We try to control them by classifying the wards according to level of need." He admits that gang activity is as prevalent within the CYA as it is on the streets.

I ask to speak privately with a Preston ward.

We walk to one of the dormitory units and enter the front room, a recreation center. There is a television in the corner, a ping-pong table folded against a far wall and a row of cushioned chairs lining the rest of the room.

Three counselors — two men and a woman — greet the staff member as he enters the room. He tells them of my request to speak with a ward.

They walk a kid out of his solitary cell. I extend my hand. It's an unusual and strained situation for everyone involved.

"Five minutes," the staff member says.

We move to two chairs at the side of the room.

The ward is a black youth, 17 years old. He's big for his age. He stares over my left shoulder. I try to catch his gaze. He shifts it to the right. I ask him how he arrived at Preston.

"I was 13 when I got caught for burglary," he says, slowly. "There was this toy store that had these remote-control cars, and I wanted them. I got in there at night and took all but five of them. I got 23, and I was going to sell them. I didn't get caught until my brothers started saying, 'Take us there! Take us there!' You know how kids are.

"So, I took them there, and we got caught, and I did a month at [. . .] and then went to [. . .] because I was messing up. I got board-ordered [by the CYA board] to a treatment program at [. . .] but I didn't like it there because I was so far from home. After about a year, they got tired of me and sent me here."

I ask him if he's seen or experienced any kind of physical abuse within the CYA. He glances at the staff standing at the front counter, across the room. He looks back at me and nods.

"There's always one dude who likes to beat guys up. We got one here."

I ask if he's seen or experienced any kind of sexual abuse within the CYA. "Sure," he says. "[A staff member] here likes some of the guys."

I ask the ward to write the name of the counselor on a piece of paper. He declines.

Later, I am allowed to speak privately with a young man who says he's served three years in the CYA. He's at the end of his sentence and soon expects to rejoin the outside world.

"Gladiator school," he says. "That's all it is. Me, I'm lucky. I got my head on straight. Any kind of help I got here, I did on my own. The [programs] they talk about got nothing to do with it. Truth is, not many of these guys are going to make it out of here."

As people become aware of the abuses within our juvenile correction institutions — and the cyclical nature of victim to criminal — Dwight Abbott and I now offer a few suggestions for how to cope with these most dismal problems.

Every incarcerated child needs a secure, comfortable room

where he can be left alone with his thoughts, withdrawing when necessary from the pressures inherent to any open dormitory living situation. As they are now designed, institutional facilities only dehumanize and depersonalize the wards. The "rehabilitants" are instilled with a sense of futility and alienation, likely leading to further expressions of violent, sociopathic behavior.

A strict policy needs to be instituted for the hiring and review of all juvenile institution staff. Those inclined towards sadism and other sexual pathologies should not be left in the care of troubled youth.

Finally, the authors of this book advocate the need for love and support of America's children. All evils are acquired. Every child begins in innocence.

# SELECTED BIBLIOGRAPHY

Listed below are significant books and articles on the subjects of child abuse and juvenile incarceration.

"Abusive Children," *Psychology Today,* September 1985.

Ambrosiano, Lillian, *Runaways,* Beacon Press, 1971.

"America's Troubled Children," A series of reports by *The Christian Science Monitor,* September 1988.

Cole, Larry, *Our Children's Keeper,* Grossman Publishers, 1972.

Cooney, Judy, *Coping with Sexual Abuse,* Rosen, 1987.

DeCourcy, Peter and Judith, *A Silent Tragedy: Child Abuse in the Community,* Alfred Publishing, 1973.

Ennew, Judith, *The Sexual Exploitation of Children,* St. Martin Press, 1986.

Garbarino, Schellenback, Sebes & Associates, *Troubled Youth — Troubled Family,* Aldine Publications, 1986.

"Hidden Histories of Death Row," *Science News,* October 1987.

Harris, Jean, *They Always Call Us Ladies,* Scribners, 1988.

James, Howard, *Children in Trouble: A National Scandal,* Pocket Books, 1971.

Kramer, Rita, *At a Tender Age: Violent Youth and Juvenile Justice,* Holt, 1988.

Lazzarino, Alex, & Hayes, E. Kent, *Find a Safe Place,* McGraw-Hill, 1984.

Lockwood, Daniel, *Prison Sexual Violence,* Elsevier, 1980.

Moore, Daniel S., *Enter Without Knocking,* University of Arizona Press, 1969.

Murphy, Patrick T., *Our Kindly Parent the State: The Juvenile Justice System and How it Works,* Viking Press, 1974.

O'Brien, Shirley, *Child Abuse: A Crying Shame*, Brigham Young, 1980.

Quinn, P.E., *Cry Out: Inside the Terrifying World of an Abused Child*, Abingdon Press, 1984.

Rasmussen, John, *Man in Isolation and Confinement*, Aldine Publishing Co., 1973.

Rawls, Windall, *Cold Storage*, Simon and Schuster, 1980.

Sankin, Daniel Jay, *Wounded Men: Healing from Childhood Abuse*, Harper & Row, 1988.

Schwartz, Ira M., *(In)Justice For Juveniles*, Lexington Books, 1989.

Street, Vinter, & Perrow, *Organization for Treatment: A Comparative Study of Institutions for Delinquents*, Free Press, 1966.

Thomas, Piri, *Down These Mean Streets*, Signet, 1958.

Tomasevski, Katharina, *Children in Adult Prisons: An International Perspective*, St. Martin, 1986.

Wooden, Kenneth, *Weeping in the Playtime of Others: America's Incarcerated Children*, McGraw-Hill, 1976.

## A Tear

A single tear on an eyelash may not fill an ocean,
But it's backed by just as much depth and emotion.
With words unspoken, it can betray your soul so clear.
It glistens like crystal, as a warning that hurt is near.
As it abandons you, it'll etch a path down your face.
As the teardrop silently falls, another's in its place.
It can be a reminder of good times or bad.
Or of happy dreams that somehow turned sad.
There are tears shed in anger, or shed with joy.
A tear can be equally shared by girl or boy.
A good cry can release built-up tension I'm told.
You never outgrow the need to cry; you're never too old.
To shed an occasional tear tells the world you care.
Like when they raise Old Glory, tears from pride we share.
To cry with Dad when he's suffering,
When there is nothing you can do.
The tears tell him you share his pain.
He'd do the same for you.

by Tommy Abbott
son of Dwight Edgar Abbott
Born: June 2, 1965
Murdered: Feb. 22, 1984

# About the Authors

**Dwight Edgar Abbott** has spent the past 38 years incarcerated within some of this country's most notorious juvenile and adult institutions, jails and prisons.

As a child, Abbott was confined to Los Angeles County Juvenile Hall, Optimist Home for Boys in Highland Park, California State Mental Hospital at Camarillo, Fred C. Nelles School for Boys, El Paso de Robles School for Boys, Preston School of Industry, Deuels Vocational Institute and, at age 17, U.S. Federal Prison at Lompoc, California.

Abbott's lengthy prison sentences have allowed him first-hand knowledge of the American penal system. As a result of his incarcerations and of the life he led outside the walls, he came to know some of this country's most infamous criminals, including Gary Gilmore, George Jackson, Charles Manson and Sirhan Sirhan.

Abbott is currently incarcerated in the California State Prison at Folsom.


**Jack Carter** received a bachelor's degree in journalism from San Diego State University in 1987. He served as a reporter and city editor for the *Daily Aztec,* the campus newspaper, and as a reporter for United Press International.

After graduation, Carter toured Mexico and Central America, writing news and shooting photographs for three U.S. newspapers. He returned to San Diego and began work for *Arete* magazine. During that time, Dwight Abbott began to correspond with Carter, seeking assistance in the completion and publication of Abbott's childhood story.

Carter continues to write books from his home in Cardiff-by-the-Sea, California.

# NOW AVAILABLE FROM FERAL HOUSE:

## *APOCALYPSE CULTURE*
## *EXPANDED AND REVISED EDITION*
### Edited by Adam Parfrey

The second edition of this underground classic has significantly fattened in size. Cultural terrorism and cutting-edge conspiracy on the death-throes of society as it approaches the third millennium. "Compulsory reading... the terminal documents of the twentieth century." — J.G. Ballard.

## *THE SECRET LIFE OF A SATANIST*
## *THE AUTHORIZED BIOGRAPHY OF ANTON LaVEY*
### By Blanche Barton

This fascinating and indispensable biography reveals what has previously been hidden from public view. Complete with documents and articles by Anton LaVey, and many never-before-published photographs. The exclusive demonography of a very dangerous man.
**CLOTH, $19.95 ISBN: 0-922915-03-2**

## *THE MAGICIAN'S DICTIONARY*
### *AN APOCALYPTIC CYCLOPÆDIA OF ADVANCED MAGI(K)AL ARTS AND ALTERNATE MEANINGS*
### By E.E. Rehmus

A trenchant, humorous and much-needed practical guide to all facets of contemporary occultism. "Surprising and delightful. I am learning from the book, something I have not said of anything since *Cosmic Trigger* and *Valis*."— James N. Martin, *Abrasax*.
**$12.95 ISBN: 0-922915-01-6**

## *THE SATANIC WITCH*
### By Anton LaVey

In this one-of-a-kind work, Anton LaVey illuminates the dynamics of erotic seduction, informed a lifetime of inspired observation, especially taken from his own carny and burlesque house adventures with rubes, Stage Door Johnnies, and sawduxt vixens. A "Satanic Witch" is a woman who knows what she wants and know how to go about getting it. Men, take special note. Introduction by Anton's bewitching daughter, Zeena.
**$9.95 ISBN: 0-922915-00-8**

## TORTURES & TORMENTS OF THE CHRISTIAN MARTYRS
### By Rev. Antonio Gallonio

The most gut-wrenching document of all time, written by a Catholic priest for the "edification" of the faithful! Included are the original 15th century woodcuts, a forensic examination of the crucifixion by M.D's at the Mayo Clinic, and dozens of amazing illuminations executed specifically for this edition by such subverts as: Peter Bagge, Joe Coleman, S. Clay Wilson, Charles Manson, Richard Ramirez, Savage Pencil, Sarita Vendetta, Crispin Glover, etc. Hurry! Supply limited.

**$12.95 ISBN: 0-922915-02-4**

# COMING IN 1991 FROM FERAL HOUSE:

## NIGHTMARE OF ECSTASY
## THE LIFE AND ART OF EDWARD D. WOOD, JR.
### By Rudolph Grey

For nearly ten years, Rudolph Grey has searched the catacombs and dregs of the film and pornography industries. The result is a photographically rich joyride through the dark side of Hollywood and its weirdest and most tragic auteur. New, incredible material on Bela Lugosi, Tor Johnson, Vampira, Criswell, and all the other quintessential Woodian characters that have made *Glen or Glenda* and *Plan 9 From Outer Space* such unforgettable experiences.

## COSMIC RETRIBUTION
## THE INFERNAL ART OF JOE COLEMAN

Joe Coleman's paintings and drawings are the most accomplished and expressive visions of personal apocalypse since Wölfli, Kahlo, Dix, and Bosch. *Cosmic Retribution* is the definitive exploration into the hemorrhaging gestalt of this contemporary genius. Large format. Many color pages.

## CAD
## A HANDBOOK FOR HEELS
### Edited by Charles Schneider

A book-length evocation of the lost era of girlie magazines. Torrid pictorials, boozology, two-fisted tales of devilish bachelorhood, all the forgotten lore of the red-blooded American male. 250 pages, large-format. Art Directed by Doug Erb. With contributions by Chet Baker, Virgil Partch, Russ Meyer, Elmer Batters, Charles Krafft, Bill Ward, Dick Blackburn, Daniel Clowes, Adam rey, Kyle Roderick, Brian Chic, Hensley, Don Kennison, Damon Runyon, Kennison, Herbert Hucke, Cliff Mott, Cooper, and Tina Louise!

## AMOK PRESS TITLES AVAILABLE FROM FERAL HOUSE

### THE MANSON FILE
A limited supply of this definitive view of Manson that the District Attorney would rather not have you see.
ISBN: 0-941693-04-X  $9.95  (Copies may be slightly damaged.)

### THE GRAND GUIGNOL: THEATRE OF FEAR AND TERROR
**Mel Gordon**
The first English language book on the famous theatre which spawned the genre of modern horror.  Oversized, extensively illustrated.
ISBN: 0-941693-08-2  $12.95

### RANTS & INCENDIARY TRACTS
**Edited by Bob Black and Adam Parfrey**
Untethered outbursts by history's most dangrous freethinkers.
ISBN: 0-941693-03-1  $9.95

### YOU CAN'T WIN: The Autobiography of Jack Black
**Foreword by William S. Burroughs**
A lost classic of American road literature vividly etched in the argot of a criminal underclass.
ISBN: 0-941693-07-4  $9.95

### BOXCAR BERTHA: An Autobiography
**As told to Dr. Ben L Reitman. Introduction by Kathy Acker.**
ISBN: 0-941693-06-6  $7.95

### MICHAEL: A Novel
**Joseph Goebbels.  Translated by Joachim Neugroschel.**
ISBN: 0-941693-00-7  $6.95

### DISNEYLAND OF THE GODS
**John A. Keel**
"Keel's books never fail to astound and delight me." — Robert Anton Wilson.
ISBN: 0-941693-05-8  $8.95